FINDING
YOUR
VERY BEST
NEXT
WORK LIFE

strategies for
successful career change

MARTHA E. MANGELSDORF

Ten Speed Press
Berkeley

Published in the United States by Ten Speed Press, an imprint of the Crown
Publishing Group, a division of Random House, Inc., New York.
www.crownpublishing.com
www.tenspeed.com

Ten Speed Press and the Ten Speed Press colophon are registered trademarks of
Random House, Inc.

Library of Congress Cataloging-in-Publication Data

Mangelsdorf, Martha E.
  Strategies for successful career change : finding your very best next work life /
Martha E. Mangelsdorf.
     p. cm.
  Includes bibliographical references and index.
  Summary: "A practical guide to changing careers, including tips, exercises, and
resources to help readers navigate the logistical, financial, and emotional challenges of career transition"—Provided by publisher.
  1. Career changes—United States. 2. Vocational guidance—United States.
3. Job hunting—United States. I. Title.
  HF5384.M34 2009
  650.140973—dc22
                          2009002365

  ISBN-13: 978-1-58008-824-4
  ISBN-10: 1-58008-824-4

Printed in the United States of America on recycled paper (30% PCW)

Design by Betsy Stromberg

10 9 8 7 6 5 4 3 2 1

First Edition

This book is dedicated to my wonderful husband,
Roy, the light of my life, and to Max, my beloved stepson.
It is also dedicated to my parents, Mary and Paul, who taught me
the great joy that comes from learning and gaining knowledge.

contents

acknowledgments

Thanks to all the many career-changers who shared their stories and experiences so willingly with me, often in multiple interviews conducted over a period of years. Although not everyone's story appears in the book, all were helpful and informative. Thanks, too, to all of the career-changers' friends, family, and former colleagues who also allowed me to interview them during the course of the four years I wrote a newspaper series about career change.

Thank you to all the many talented and capable individuals at Ten Speed Press, for their skill, gifts, and hard work at all phases of the book's production. In particular, I want to thank my editor, Brie Mazurek, whose insights have been terrific, skillful, and helpful; editorial director Aaron Wehner; copyeditor Kristi Hein; and designer Betsy Stromberg. Thanks also to my agent, Colleen Mohyde, for her excellent advice throughout this process.

I have worked with many great editors over the years, but I would particularly like to thank Steff Gelston. Steff, a senior editor at CXO Media, is a former assistant business editor of the *Boston Globe* newspaper, where she edited the paper's Sunday careers section. Steff was the editor to whom I wrote my initial proposal for the "Transitions" series, and she was my editor for most of the time I wrote that freelance series for the *Globe*. I can't thank her enough for being such a great editor: open to new ideas, full of good feedback and perspective—and kind and efficient, as well.

Special thanks also go to my brother, Paul Mangelsdorf III, and my sister-in-law Laurice, for their exceptional support. I am particularly blessed that Laurice—a former financial aid counselor—was willing to volunteer her time to help me research complex financial aid issues as background material for the chapter on training. Thank you, Laurice.

Thanks to all the many people who have helped me at various stages in the process of conceiving and writing this book. In particular, I received very helpful advice or feedback early on from a number of successful book authors: Bo Burlingham, Donna Fenn, Jeffrey Seglin, and Lan Samantha Chang. Special thanks go to my friend and former boss Diane Franklin for her invaluable coaching. Thanks also to several people who were available at one point or another to do small freelance coaching, research, or filing projects related to the book: Jaffray Cuyler, for her excellent coaching during one phase of the writing; Amy E. Davidson, for her help in researching the Resources box in chapter 10; and Sierra Roseboro, for her help in setting up an article archive.

Thanks to the following people who served on a "clearness committee" (a Quaker process for helping individuals reach spiritual discernment about a life decision of some type) that I convened in 2007 to consider a question related to the book: Penny Yunuba, Margaret Benefiel, Patrick Gabridge, and Patricia Wild were all generous with their time and insights. Thanks also to my dear friend Judy Goldberger, who not only allowed me to add her story to this book but who has always offered encouragement and who has helped keep me spiritually grounded throughout this project. Thanks to Roy, my beloved husband, for his tremendous love and support throughout this challenging process. And thanks to my dear stepson, Max, for pushing me toward progress through that persistent question of his: "How's the book?"

introduction

I saw that there is nothing better for a man
than to enjoy his work, because that is his lot.
—Ecclesiastes 3:22

This is a book about finding work you enjoy. If you're thinking about changing careers but aren't sure how to do it, this book is for you. If you've ever read or heard about people who've changed careers and wondered how they went about doing it, this book should help. It's a book about the "how" of career change—one that grew out of in-depth interviews with dozens of people who have successfully changed careers. It's about how to do research about a new career, how to test career possibilities in low-risk ways, and how to juggle money and family issues. It's about how to follow your dreams but still pay the bills. Whether you are seriously thinking about changing careers or just exploring the idea a little, *Strategies for Successful Career Change* can help.

However, if you dream of a perfect new career—one that will fulfill all your dreams for work and be without problems or drawbacks—this book may disappoint you. Work is seldom, if ever, perfect. And no career will be without problems or drawbacks. As I interviewed career-changers, it became abundantly clear that career change is hard work, often takes a long time—and is somewhat risky. What's more, although finding more satisfying work can definitely improve your happiness and the quality of your life, changing careers is unlikely to make you happy if you tend to be a chronically unhappy person.

But if you are thinking realistically about changing careers—and need down-to-earth, practical information about how real people do that—this book is for you. In my talks with successful career-changers, I identified certain patterns and themes that were part of a number of people's experiences. Although no one career-changer fits all the patterns, I could nonetheless see themes and best practices that emerged in various career-changers' stories. Throughout this book I'll share their stories, with an emphasis on how they made the transition successfully.

why I wrote this book

My introduction to the art of career change came through my own experience of career transition. In my twenties and early thirties, I was truly blessed in my work. I had found work that really fit me at the time, and I loved it. (It wasn't perfect, but I think it was as close to perfect as work gets.) In college I had been torn between becoming an economist or a newspaper reporter; I had majored in economics yet also loved being a reporter and editor at my college's daily paper. Ultimately, I blended both interests and became a business journalist. I soon landed, in my mid-twenties, as a reporter/researcher at *Inc.* magazine, the nation's leading magazine about running and growing a small business.

Inc. and I were a perfect fit. I was passionate about small businesses, and, in an era when large corporations could no longer be relied on for employment stability, I believed that it was extremely important to help people learn how to start and run their own businesses better; it seemed extraordinarily important to our economy and to people's lives to convey good, solid, practical information about how to start, manage, and grow a business. There was nothing I, as a journalist, wanted to do more; I couldn't imagine a better job.

For many years, I prospered at *Inc.* magazine, getting promoted regularly, becoming a senior writer and ultimately a senior editor. But after about a decade, I started to get itchy. I was a bit of a workaholic at the time, and as a result, I felt like my work ran my life. The professional fast track that had felt fun in my twenties was starting to feel like a trap by my mid-thirties. I wanted more time for volunteer work and personal growth, and I wondered if I would ever have time and energy to find a mate and have a family of my own. (I eventually did meet my mate, but not until after I'd left that job and created a more balanced life.) Sometimes I felt like a hamster running hard in a wheel. Professionally, I was so consumed by my job that it was hard to think what other work I might want to do. But I was beginning to burn out at my job, and I knew in my soul it was time for something to change.

I didn't know what to do, but I somehow felt having more time to myself would help. I first sought to reduce my work hours to work four-fifths time, with a corresponding reduction in salary, but my boss wasn't receptive to that idea. Because I had figured out a way to reduce my income requirements some, I got the courage to leave my job for a combination of part-time and freelance work. I even, in effect, became a career-changer, although ultimately my own career change proved temporary. You see, I was so passionate about small business that, instead of leaving the small-business magazine where I worked to go to another journalism job (which would have been a more standard career move), I took a less-than-full-time job at a nonprofit that helped people start and grow businesses, and I supplemented that job with a freelance editing project. My nonprofit job let me learn new skills (something that I was itching to do): instead of writing and editing, I managed programs and events for people who were starting and growing high-tech companies.

My career change to that nonprofit organization ultimately proved to be a temporary one, but I'll never forget how scary it was to walk away voluntarily from my fairly prestigious magazine job to try a new kind of work. I felt like I was walking away from the career and workplace around which I had built a successful professional identity; at the time, I didn't know who I was professionally without the workplace where I'd been successful. From that experience, I empathize with the difficult decisions that can surround career change.

In the long term, though, my temporary career change experiment—which lasted about a year—proved to be a good move for me. Working in a nonprofit was a great experience of reinventing myself in a new venue. By leaving my magazine job, I gained new connections, new contacts, new maturity, and new skills; in fact, when I later worked for a number of years as a self-employed writer and editor, I found that I frequently worked on writing or editing projects that could be traced back, indirectly, to contacts I made during that year at the nonprofit, when I was experimenting with career change. And because I was also freelancing part-time as an editor during that year, I was learning about self-employment firsthand, rather than just through books and interviews.

Then, after about a year, I unexpectedly returned to *Inc.* when a tempting job offer came up that would let me learn new Internet-publishing skills while working for the website affiliated with *Inc.*, www.inc.com. In 2000, while I was working for the website, *Inc.* magazine's founder and owner, Bernie Goldhirsh, was diagnosed with a brain tumor and needed to sell *Inc.* (Sadly, Bernie—as he was affectionately known throughout the company—passed away in 2003.) And less than a year after *Inc.* was sold in 2000, I was laid off, along with many others who worked at the magazine's website; later, *Inc.* moved its editorial headquarters to another city.

Worse yet, my layoff happened just as a recession was starting in early 2001. In Massachusetts, the state where I live, the information-technology economy was in free fall after the Internet boom of the late 1990s became a bust; Massachusetts lost more than 6 percent of its non-farm jobs during that recession and the years immediately following it—more, percentage-wise, than any other state in the nation during that time.[1] In that environment, I decided to launch my own business, as a self-employed writer and editor. It was an unsettling time—and having gone through that experience, when I talk to people who have changed careers after experiencing the trauma of being downsized, I empathize with that experience, too.

But in that recession I also saw something interesting. All around me I saw people who were changing careers, often because they had to. Others, although not changing careers, were nonetheless managing major career transitions much as I was—doing things like learning to build a business as a self-employed person rather than as an employee. Yet most of us had little training in how to change careers or even how to manage a major career transition in the same industry; after all, nobody had ever asked us when we were kids what *variety of things* we wanted to be when we grew up! The assumption most of us grew up with—that we would have one, fairly linear career—was being turned upside down, right in front of us. And I saw people having to make fairly dramatic changes in their work lives without access to much good information about how to make a career change.

I knew from my many years at *Inc.* magazine that one of the ways adults learn best is through hearing other people's stories; at *Inc.*, we specialized in telling entrepreneurs' stories in ways that other entrepreneurs could learn from. So I decided to try to do the same thing for career-changers: to tell the stories of successful ones so that others could learn from them. I was freelancing at the time for the Sunday careers section of the *Boston Globe* newspaper, and I wrote a proposal to the then editor of that section for a new monthly series that I would write, profiling people who had made significant changes in their careers and emphasizing how they did it.

My editor liked my proposal, and for the next four years I profiled people who had made career changes in a monthly series called "Transitions" that ran in the *Globe*. Given my years of training as a how-to business reporter with a focus on finding and conveying practical information, along the way I began to spot trends and patterns among the more than fifty interviews I conducted with the career-changers I wrote about in that series and in other articles. I also saw many useful tips and ideas that other people could learn from in the career-changers' stories— and often, given space constraints, I couldn't fit those tips and trends into my freelance articles. (That was in part because, for the career change series, I made it a habit to interview and quote not only the person changing careers but also people who knew him or her, such as the person's spouse or former colleagues. That added perspective and depth to my articles—but took up space.) Over time, those patterns, trends, tips, and ideas that I knew could help others inspired me to write this book, and eventually I stopped writing the freelance series for the *Globe* in order to make more time available to research and write this book. The result is a book grounded in how real people, from all walks of life, successfully make substantial changes in their careers.

the serendipity factor

One fascinating factor in career transition is the role of serendipity— of things you don't plan but that just occur or evolve as you interact with life. William Bridges, one of the foremost experts on life transitions, puts it beautifully in his book *The Way of Transition: Embracing Life's Most Difficult Moments*. At one point in that book, Bridges compares his own experience of developing his career to walking in a natural landscape, where the process is "more like following the contours of the land" than following a set path.[2] And, he notes, whatever you undertake, "the actual result, the lesson or the payoff, is discovered only over time, and often in ways that you could not have known in advance." Bridges also observes that your path in life itself provides you with "cues" that can influence your career direction.[3]

That's certainly been my experience. I'm a Quaker by religion, and, given my growing interest in career transition back in 2001, it's probably not surprising that I began noticing people in my Quaker congregation (called a "Quaker meeting") who were out of work during the recession then under way—but our congregation had no formal mechanism to help people with career issues. So I started a support group at my Quaker meeting for people in any type of career transition; it's called Friends in Career Transition, and for seven years I've served as that twice-monthly group's volunteer facilitator.

When I started Friends in Career Transition, I had no intention of writing a book about career change; starting the support group was a classic case of what Bridges describes as taking a "cue" from the path in life you find yourself on. But serendipitously, through that volunteer work, I've had the opportunity to listen to the stories of dozens of people as they were right in the middle of a variety of career transitions, from job-hunting to contemplating career change. Those private stories are not included in this book, of course, but they definitely ended up helping me once I decided to write a book. Listening to people's experiences with career transition as those experiences were unfolding helped me to much better understand the wide range of issues that people may cope with during periods of career transition—from concerns about paying the bills to uncertainty about the future.

how to use this book

Strategies for Successful Career Change is designed to be of practical use, so I've structured the book in a way that I hope makes it easier for busy people to use and access. Instead of, say, eight or nine long chapters, you'll find eighteen short ones, each a length you can read in a short chunk of time—the kind of chunk you might be able to spare early in the morning, before going to sleep at night, while waiting for a bus or train or appointment, over a cup of coffee or tea, while your small child takes a nap, or while you are eating lunch during the workday. You don't have to read this book all at once (although you certainly can), and in fact you may get the most use out of it if you read it gradually. The reason? Each chapter addresses a different topic that many career-changers need to consider. And the chapters generally include not only examples from people's real-life career change experiences, but also questions for you to consider and other resources you can explore. If you choose to read the book bit by bit, you'll have more time to explore the questions and resources and think about them. (But if the best way for you to read the book is in one fell swoop on a rainy Sunday afternoon, or during a vacation, or on a long trip, that's a good approach also.)

Although this book is designed to be read in its entirety, most of the chapters stand on their own, too. So if, as you read the table of contents, you find yourself truly drawn to a particular chapter, feel free to start the book there. For most people, reading the book from start to finish will make most sense. But let's face it: we all have, in our life-times, started some books that we haven't finished reading. That's a missed opportunity. If the questions addressed by certain chapters of this book are not terribly relevant to your situation, you can skim or skip them for now and spend more time on the ones that best address your current needs. In all the chapters, you'll find Resources boxes that list useful books, articles, or websites. You can find links to the online resources at the book's website, www.strategiesforcareerchange.com.

mastering the art of career change

I wish I could tell you that if you read this book, do all the exercises faithfully, and follow all the steps, you'll find a career that will satisfy you for the rest of your working life. Unfortunately, in today's economy I can't promise that. We live, for better or worse, in a society full of unprecedented change, much of it technology-driven. As technologies come and go, so do companies, jobs, and careers. As a result, it's very hard to predict how anyone's career will unfold over the rest of his or her working life: the pace of change is too fast—and too unpredictable—in our modern society. Who would have dreamed twenty-five years ago, for example, that a new technology called the Internet would open up all kinds of new opportunities—but also lead to declines in the economic prospects of fields as diverse as newspapers and stores selling music albums?

> If the questions addressed by certain chapters of this book are not terribly relevant to your situation, you can skim or skip them for now and spend more time on the chapters that best address your current needs.

The prospect of constant change—and no guarantee of a safe career—is a frightening one. In truth, the whole idea of career change can be scary. Who wants to start out as a newcomer in something, when you've already built up skills and a reputation in one line of work? The unpleasant truth, however, is that if you don't change careers now, you may have to some time in the future. (And of course, even if you do change careers now, you may decide—or need—to do so again later!)

So if you find the idea of career change intriguing but daunting, don't think about it only as leaving behind what you already know. Think about it as learning an important new skill, one that will help you for the rest of your life: the skill of career transition. There is an art to career change, and although the process is challenging, there are steps you can take to make it more manageable. And once you learn the skill of managing career transitions, you can be less fearful—and more resilient—in your economic future. As you read this book, you are not just learning about how to change careers; you're also learning how to better navigate periods of change and economic transition. And that is a strength that you can carry with you for the rest of your working life.

Martha E. Mangelsdorf
www.strategiesforcareerchange.com

PART I

TAKING STOCK

In this first section of the book, the focus is all on you. You'll be asked to consider why you want to change careers and what you want from life, and you'll get ideas about how you can gain a new perspective on your career. You'll also think through how money matters and your personal and family life affect the practical realities of your own situation. You'll have a chance to contemplate some big questions, like what's been missing from your work life so far, and what role your personal aspirations and spiritual life may play in your career transition.

The goal? *To think through what you really want and need from work, so that you can make decisions that are right for you.*

why do you want to change careers?

Congratulations! Many—perhaps most—people in contemporary society think about changing careers sometimes, and lots of people really wish they could but don't know how. Others feel forced by changing economic or personal circumstances to consider a new career. But even when you feel you might benefit from doing a different kind of work, career change can seem hard, impractical, or downright overwhelming— simply too intimidating a project to undertake.

That's why I congratulate you. By reading this book you're doing two important things:

1. You're exploring some interest you have in career change, rather than just feeling stuck.

2. By gathering more information, you're also taking a very practical, low-risk step toward investigating the topic of possible career change.

As you'll discover in this book, one smart strategy for career-changers is to start with low-risk research and small steps that give you more information. As you read this book and consider the topics it raises, you're starting that kind of gradual, thoughtful exploration process.

why people change careers

If you're thinking about changing careers, you're not alone. There are all kinds of reasons people start a new career, and career change has become increasingly accepted in our society. For one thing, ours is a society built on rapid technological change, and both organizations and the markets they serve come and go in response to economic, technological, and societal changes. Then, too, an increasingly global economy has led to the loss of many jobs to foreign competition, as once-secure jobs have been offshored or outsourced, or both. Unfortunately, when such sweeping changes occur, many individual workers find themselves adrift—cut off from the organizations and careers in which they once worked, and needing to reinvent themselves.

What's more, work today is often unsatisfying. The world of work—particularly in the 24-7, always-on global economy—has not always adjusted well to fit the needs of families with both parents working outside the home—or, for that matter, the needs of the single person who wants to have a meaningful life beyond work. As a result, many people want to create new careers that better suit their lifestyles. Still others decide to try another kind of work because they really long to do something different from their first career, or they just, for whatever reason, feel frustrated or unhappy with their existing jobs. Finally, many people in our society are living longer and healthier lives—and many older adults, for a variety of reasons, would prefer to start new careers rather than either completely retire or remain in their current jobs.

Whatever the factors behind your interest in exploring career change, there are a number of questions you should consider; this book is organized around eighteen such questions. And you can gain many insights from a wide variety of people who've successfully changed careers—which is why lessons from such people are an integral part of this book. Whether you're changing careers in your twenties or your fifties, with a high school diploma or with a graduate degree, while raising a family or while on your own as a single adult, you can learn from others who have done something similar.

However, changing careers is usually not easy; in fact, doing so often takes a lot of work. It also can be risky; there's no guarantee of success. So as you start exploring your questions about career change, it's helpful to begin by thinking through the factors driving your interest in the subject, as well as any alternatives to career change that might meet your needs.

> As you start exploring your questions about career change, it's helpful to begin by thinking through the factors driving your interest in the subject, as well as any alternatives to career change that might meet your needs.

Although there are elements common to different types of career changes, there are also differences—depending on the reasons you're considering a new career. That's why one of the first questions to think about is what is driving your interest in changing the kind of work you do. Which of the following statements are true for you? Choose as many as apply; for many people, there are multiple factors contributing to their interest in a new career.

A. There are changes happening right now in my industry or at the organization where I work or have worked—and the changes aren't good, from my perspective. I am concerned about future opportunities in my field. I may have been laid off, or perhaps I worry that if I stay in this job I may get laid off in the coming years.

B. I am really not happy with my current work and/or some aspect of the lifestyle that accompanies it (such as hours, pressure, risk of injury, or wages). I may or may not have enjoyed this work in the past, but I don't want to keep doing it now.

C. There is some other kind of work I'd really like to do; I'd like to pursue a dream of mine.

D. I feel that if I could only get more education and training—or switch into a higher-paying field—I could earn a better income. That's an important goal for me and would improve my quality of life.

E. I used to like my work reasonably well, but the work no longer suits me because of some change in my own life. (The particular circumstances could vary, from needing to leave a physically demanding job after an injury, to wanting to work fewer hours while caring for small children—or, on the other hand, needing to earn more because of a need to support children financially.)

F. I've accomplished all I wanted to in my current career—and now, after many years in this line of work, I want to try something different. I'm getting older, and I'd like to spend my remaining years working at something satisfying, whether on a part-time or full-time basis.

what your answers indicate

What do your answers to this mini-quiz signify? Well, different issues and questions may be more or less important to explore as you consider changing the kind of work you do—depending on what is motivating you.

For example, people for whom statement A is true are **Responding to Change in the Economy**.

If, on the other hand, you answered yes to statement B, you are **Ready to Move On**.

What if you answered yes to statement C? In that case, you are **Exploring a Dream**.

If you answered yes to statement D, you are **Eager to Move Up**.

For those who answered yes to statement E, **Things Have Changed** for you.

And, if you answered yes to statement F, you are **Looking for a Later-Stage Career**.

If you're thinking about a career change and one or more of these statements apply, here are some of the issues that may affect you.

statement a: responding to change in the economy

The good news is: If statement A is true for you, you're not being blind to the change occurring around you. You're proactively evaluating your options, which is smart. Also, you have probably developed skills in your current career that you can transfer to whatever work you do next. And if you've been happy and successful in the past doing one type of work, you may well find that you can be happy and successful in the future doing some other type of work, as well. You may also find that you don't need to make a dramatic career change; you may be able to apply your existing skill set to another industry or a closely related type of work.

Special challenges you may face: If you have been laid off or are leaving an industry because you fear for your future career prospects in that field, you may feel real grief, disorientation, or anger. It is a genuine loss to leave work you've enjoyed and that's given you an identity, and that sense of loss shouldn't be minimized—or rushed through. And if you've been working for the same company for many years, change may be particularly frightening. You may feel out of practice at the skills associated with career transition, such as networking.

resource

If statement A was true for you, and you are exploring career change because you have been laid off or fear you may be laid off in the near future, you may face an important additional task. In addition to thinking about career change, you also may need to deal with the emotional ramifications of leaving the kind of work you used to do. A good book on this subject is *Are You a Corporate Refugee? A Survival Guide for Downsized, Disillusioned, and Displaced Workers* by Ruth Luban (New York: Penguin Books, 2001). Luban, a counselor who recognized that the experience of displaced and laid-off workers had certain similarities to what her parents and grandfather experienced as immigrant refugees, wrote a book that is a comforting guide to recuperating from job loss. (If you're interested in *Are You a Corporate Refugee?* but can't find a copy, ask your local librarian if it's available via interlibrary loan.)

Also, if career change is something you're considering because of external factors—rather than because this is a good or easy time in your life to change careers—you may face real financial issues. For example, your industry may be downsizing due to technological changes or international competition—at a time when you have young children to support. Or perhaps you're currently fully employed but thinking about changing careers because you think opportunities ahead don't look good in your field; if so, finding the time to research or prepare for an alternative career may be challenging. And if you're changing careers because of external changes—rather than because you are drawn to some particular type of new career—you may need time to explore various options.

Some questions to consider as you contemplate career change:

1. Is a new position—rather than an entirely new career—an option for you?

2. Would relocation be an option in your case, or help the situation?

3. If you really like your industry, profession, or both, are there any firms or sectors of your industry or profession that are growing? Are there variations on the kind of work you do—in other words, related kinds of work—that might have good growth prospects? (You'll learn more about identifying growth markets in chapter 9.)

4. If you like your work and are good at it, are there skills you use in it that you would like to use in other work? (This topic will be covered further in chapters 4, 7, and 10.)

5. Can you give yourself time—and permission—to deal with your sense of loss? Leaving a kind of work you have enjoyed can entail real grief, and it may help to acknowledge that.

6. What kind of financial flexibility do you have to make a career transition? (This question will be discussed further in chapter 6.)

statement b: ready to move on

The good news is: If statement B is true for you, you may have more control over the timing and nature of your career-change process than if it's driven by external changes. Even though you do not like your current job (at least not anymore) and very much want to do something else, there's a good chance you have the option of starting to explore potential new careers gradually, while continuing to work at your current job. It may even be possible to try out a potential new career (or preparation for it) on a part-time basis—either in conjunction with your current full-time work, or by pursuing two careers at once, both part-time. (You'll learn more about the two-career option in chapter 14.)

Special challenges you may face: If you are primarily driven by a desire to leave your current career but are not sure what you want to do next, one challenge you face may be finding or making enough time to figure out your next move. You need to find time in your schedule to start to explore options and chart a new course for your career. You may also need to evaluate further the question of whether it's your career you dislike or just your current job.

Some questions to consider as you contemplate career change:

1. Is it possible you are unhappy with your current job or work arrangement more than with your career? Are there any circumstances in which you might be happy in your current occupation or field?

2. What is it you really don't like about your current work? What is dissatisfying about it?

3. What are some characteristics you'd like your next work arrangement to have?

4. How can you create some time to learn about other possible career options in a low-risk way? (You'll learn more about this kind of research in several of the other chapters, particularly chapters 11, 12, and 13.)

statement c: exploring a dream

The good news is: If statement C is true for you, you already have a goal (or perhaps several possible goals you're deciding among). And because your goal represents something that really interests and intrigues you, that will probably make it easier to research; people tend to be naturally drawn to things that really interest them. You'll gain energy for your career explorations from your desire to do the kind of work you want to.

Special challenges you may face: Because you're enthusiastic about this goal, you need to take care to also research it thoughtfully before you go ahead—so that you don't later find yourself disappointed by some aspect of your new career that you had overlooked. If this is a dream you've had for a while, there may be some reason you haven't pursued it earlier. It may be you just didn't have the opportunity before, but if there are real obstacles to fulfilling your dream, you need to understand and confront them. Perhaps your ideal career involves a field in which it's hard to make the kind of living you want, or perhaps the training you need to enter the career that interests you seems daunting. If you face significant hurdles in achieving your dream, you need to explore and evaluate them carefully and thoughtfully.

Some questions to consider as you contemplate career change:

1. What exactly does your ideal work consist of? What are the important elements of your dream?

2. What are the unknowns about this career—what do you need to know about what it's like to work in this occupation that you don't know yet? (Part II of this book will be of special interest to you, as it addresses different aspects of learning about careers.)

3. If your dream doesn't seem practical (for example, the training is too long, or the wages are too low), what aspects of it are most important to you? Is there a variation of your dream, or a related occupation, that might give you the elements of your dream that are most important to you? (This topic will be discussed in chapter 8.)

4. Where is there intersection between what you want to do and what people will pay you adequately for? (Chapter 8 also addresses this topic.)

5. If pursuing your dream might mean lowering your income— either temporarily, while in transition, or long-term—is that a trade-off that you (and your spouse, if you are married) are willing to consider? (Chapter 6 will help you think through that question.)

statement d: eager to move up

The good news is: If statement D is true for you, there's a kind of work you really want to do that is in demand and that pays more than what you currently earn. That's in many ways the best of all possible worlds. It's a goal that your friends and family may well support, at least in the abstract. Odds are good that you won't have to spend a lot of time explaining to other people why you're pursuing this kind of career change; people will often understand and applaud your desire to both earn more and do work you'd like to do. And the twin goals of earning more and pursuing a career that interests you are likely to be motivating to you as you explore career change.

Special challenges you may face: You need to look carefully into the field you're considering, to find out about whether it will indeed yield the opportunities you hope for and whether you'll enjoy the work. If you're considering additional schooling, one issue you'll have to analyze thoughtfully is the costs versus the likely future benefits of any additional training or education you think you may need. And you'll need to do lots of research on any training program or schooling you're considering before you put down any money or take out any loans. You don't want to end up owing money for schooling that wasn't useful. Also, if you are pursuing education or training while working, raising a family, or both, you'll have a lot of juggling to do, in terms of both time and money. You'll need to consider the sacrifices up front, both for yourself and for your family.

Some questions to consider as you contemplate career change:

1. Are you confident that the field that interests you will have good opportunities for you? (You'll learn more about researching and exploring careers in part II.)

2. How can you figure out whether any training or schooling you are considering is a good investment? Are there alternatives to getting formal schooling, such as informal apprenticeships or on-the-job training? (Chapter 15 will discuss this topic.)

3. Is the career you're contemplating a good fit with your existing education and skills? For example, if you're considering going to law school, are you skilled at writing and reading? Or, if you're contemplating a career that requires you to work well with your hands, is that something you're good at?

4. How much debt would you have to take on to get any additional training you're considering? How long would it take you to pay it off?

statement e: things have changed

The good news is: If statement E is true for you, you were previously reasonably satisfied in your career. That's a good sign, because it suggests that—as a person who can be happy in his or her work—you have a good chance of being happy again. You also have a strong motivation to change careers, because something about your previous work really doesn't work for you anymore. Yet you may be able to transfer skills and interests from your previous career to whatever you do next.

Special challenges you may face: You may have mixed emotions about changing careers, particularly if the change that has affected you has an external source, such as an injury or illness that prevents you from doing what you used to do. And, like those career-changers who are primarily driven by external changes such as downsizing, you may need to spend some time figuring out what to do next and exploring your options.

Some questions to consider as you contemplate career change:

1. In the past, what did you like best about the work you did?

2. In what ways would you like your new work to be similar to your old work? Are there skills and interests you'd like to continue to use?

3. What needs to be different in your next career, from your perspective?

4. What are the characteristics of an ideal work arrangement for this stage of your life?

5. Is it possible to have that type of work arrangement and stay in your current industry?

statement f: looking for a later-stage career

The good news is: If statement F is true for you, this may be a great time of life to explore new career options. If you are financially secure, you can pursue work you find particularly satisfying, and this really *is* a time when you can follow your career dreams. And if you still need to earn a good salary, you may nonetheless have fewer financial responsibilities to others, if your children have grown up and left home. In any case, you are wiser, more experienced—and more likely to know what you want out of your remaining years at work. These are all advantages you can use in contemplating a career change.

Special challenges: You may face age discrimination as you try to enter a new field. There is lots of bias against older people in our culture, and it may crop up as you change careers. It shouldn't stop you, but you may have to work around it. And you may have less physical energy than the last time you were starting a new career; you may be less likely to want to stay up late working or studying, for example. Also, you may feel like you're losing part of your identity when you leave a career in which you are well established.

Some questions to consider:

1. What do you really want out of the rest of your working life? (Chapter 2, which addresses setting life goals, can help with this question, too.)

2. How much money do you need or want to earn? (Chapter 6 discusses this topic further.)

3. How can you use skills from your previous work life in the new type of work you'd like to do? (Chapter 10 looks at that question.)

what works for you?

Whatever type or combination of types you are, keep your particular advantages and challenges in mind as you read through this book. People in all kinds of different circumstances successfully change careers; there is no right or wrong time to change careers. What's important is understanding your own circumstances, talents, and goals—and making choices that work for you.

Start a career change journal. It can be any kind of notebook (the inexpensive kind you get in a drugstore is fine), but it's good if it's at least 8.5 by 11 inches in size. That way, it's big enough that you can staple in pages and papers that interest you, if you like. It will also help to start a file folder, in whatever filing system you like to use, to keep material related to your career explorations and research. If you prefer keeping all your notes electronically rather than on paper, create a computer file folder for your career change research.

You can use your career change journal to keep track of what you're thinking and feeling as you explore career change, as well as information you learn along the way, progress you make, and obstacles you encounter. You can customize the journal any way you like: if you're an artist, you can leave room for illustrations; if you're religious, include space for prayers and devotional texts that have meaning for you at this time in your life. Anything that speaks to you is fine. Allow yourself to see your thoughts and progress as you move forward. Don't worry about writing style, punctuation, or grammar: write for yourself, not for some critical English teacher you remember from your youth! It's fine to just jot down phrases and notes with important information, if you don't like to write.

Consider the alternatives. Because career change is a big undertaking, it's good to start by considering not only career change, but alternatives to it as well. Let's recap some of the questions raised in this chapter that address alternatives to career change:

- Is a new position—rather than an entirely new career—an option for you? Would relocation be an option in your case, or help the situation?

- Is it possible you are unhappy with your current job or work arrangement more than with your career? Are there any circumstances in which you might be happy in your current occupation or field?

- What are the characteristics of an ideal work arrangement for this stage of your life? Is it possible to have that type of work arrangement and stay in your current industry?

Are any of those questions relevant to your situation? If so, take some time to write down or think about your responses to them.

what do you want to accomplish before you die?

Yikes! "What do you want to accomplish before you die?" can be a scary question. In our fast-paced modern culture, we don't like to think about death—about life inevitably coming to an end. We focus instead on progress, on the next new thing.

But look at it this way. Have you ever begun a project—whether at work, in school, or at home—for which you didn't plan well and as a result ended up not accomplishing everything you wanted with the time frame and resources you had available? After the project was completed, you probably had some regrets. Is life all that different? You only get one chance to live your life. And it is, without question, the biggest project you'll ever undertake.

The funny thing is that many of us do surprisingly little planning of our biggest projects: our lives. Instead, we all too often get caught up in the day-to-day—which is particularly easy to do given the frenetic pace of much of contemporary society. We e-mail, we commute, we multi-task, we take calls on our cell phones, we type feverishly into laptops, we drop the kids off at daycare or sports practice or school, we take care of our homes, and we put bread on the table, and, hopefully, money in the bank. In all that rush, we may plan for our next vacation, our next remodeling project, our next job, our retirement finances—but not our own, personal, big-picture goals for what we want to accomplish in our remaining time on earth.

That's too bad, because if we set goals, it's more likely we'll achieve them. Now, of course, it's wise to have a little humility about your life goals. There is an old saying to the effect that "If you want to see God laugh, show Him your plans." And there's probably some truth to that. None of us know where life will lead us, so it's wise to be both adaptive and flexible.

Nonetheless, there is enormous power in setting goals. In his popular book *Never Eat Alone*, entrepreneur Keith Ferrazzi goes so far as to declare that all the successful people he's met have "in varying degrees, a zeal for goal setting."[1] Knowing what you want out of the rest of your life is important for everyone. But if you're contemplating a career change, it's a particularly pressing question, because it can help you better evaluate whatever options you're considering.

changing direction—gradually

Changing the direction of your career is a little like turning a big ship in a quite different direction: you can't do it instantly. Instead, it takes time and a steady focus on making the change to achieve a significant alteration in the ship's direction. Similarly, if you want to change the direction of your career significantly, you probably can't do it overnight; it'll be a change in course that you achieve gradually, over time. Having goals about the kind of life you want to lead will help you stay focused on the changes you want to make—and help you counteract the forces of inertia that might otherwise keep you moving in the direction in which you were previously going. For that reason, goals are particularly important if you're contemplating a voluntary career change that involves leaving full-time work you're currently doing, as the time and energy required by your current work is probably considerable—and you need strong motivations to help you make a change.

In his beautiful book *Crossing the Unknown Sea: Work as a Pilgrimage of Identity*, poet David Whyte tells a story from his own life that illustrates the power of setting goals—and taking small steps toward them—in achieving career change. While working at a nonprofit, Whyte increasingly found himself drawn toward what is without question a truly tough career choice: poetry. At some point, Whyte decided he wanted to work full-time as a poet—a daunting task. And he resolved that, to achieve his goal, he would try to do at least one thing a day that would move him toward that goal. He also began telling people about his goal of becoming a poet full-time.

One thing a day may not sound like much. But over the course of many days, the little things add up. After less than three months of daily small actions, one of those actions led to Whyte getting a chance to fill in at the last minute for a speaker who had had to cancel at a conference. At the conference, Whyte got an opportunity to speak about poetry—a speech that helped launch a new career for him.[2] But it was a series of small steps, traceable back to his own expressed goal, that helped Whyte initiate the kind of change he wanted.

> Setting goals for your life as a whole may help to orient you, over time, toward a new career direction—even if you don't know exactly what kind of career change you plan to make.

Unlike Whyte, however, many people contemplating career change *don't* yet know what they want to do next. Surprisingly, setting goals for your life as a whole may help to orient you, over time, toward a new career direction—even if you don't know exactly what kind of career change you plan to make. There are at least two reasons for this: (1) working toward your life goals may open you to new experiences, and (2) setting a goal can help you make difficult or unconventional decisions.

life goals can be a catalyst for change

Duncan McDougall is someone whose life goals led him to new experiences. Bright and talented, McDougall got an MBA in his twenties and began working at a big management consulting firm in 1987. That set him on a certain kind of fast-track career path that included high pay and long hours—a kind of career track that can be hard to leave.

But McDougall was unusual. During his early twenties, he had made a list of things he wanted to do in his life; they ranged from learning to kayak to traveling around the world. And he began to try to accomplish some of his life goals. To achieve his goal of traveling, McDougall took a leave of absence from the consulting firm in 1991 and traveled the world alone for a year. In his travels, McDougall spent lots of time in developing countries, visiting more than twenty countries in Africa, Asia, and the Middle East.

McDougall ultimately returned to his work at the consulting firm for several more years, but the trip had changed his perspective. He explained, "I came back realizing how incredibly fortunate I was in so many different ways"—such as education, quality of life, and health. He started feeling that he wanted to give back to society more. At some point after his return to consulting, McDougall began feeling he'd been consulting long enough, and he started to think about what new career path might really inspire him. He also did some volunteer tutoring with a refugee family.

One day during this period, it struck McDougall how much of his time was spent reading and writing—and he thought about what his life would be like if, like some Americans, he had very limited reading and writing skills. He began thinking about how much of an impact one could have on children's lives by helping them develop better literacy skills. Over time, while still working at the consulting firm, McDougall developed a model for a nonprofit organization he wanted to start, one that would promote a love of reading among children in rural New Hampshire and Vermont—places he had come to love while attending business school in New Hampshire. In 1997, in his mid-thirties, McDougall moved to northern New England, where in 1998 he cofounded the Children's Literacy Foundation with a team of experts. In northern New England, McDougall also met the woman who became his wife; they now live in Waterbury Center, Vermont. There McDougall is the executive director of the Children's Literacy Foundation (www .clifonline.org), which runs a variety of programs that promote a love of reading and writing among rural and at-risk children—programs such as donating new children's books to homeless shelters and low-income housing developments and helping rural public libraries buy children's books. It's quite different from working as a high-powered management consultant in the business world—but McDougall's own inner sense of what he wanted to do in his life helped give him the perspective that led him to choose a new course.

The job McDougall does now was not on his list of goals as a young man. However, the process of setting those goals and working to achieve them helped change McDougall's perspective on his life—and that, in turn, helped lead him to later make changes in his work life. And after running the Children's Literacy Foundation for a number of years, McDougall still loves his job.

goals can help you make unconventional decisions

It's hard to change—and it's easier to keep doing whatever it is you're already doing. Setting a goal is making an announcement to yourself that you want to do something different. That, in turn, will make it easier to make a change. For example, Hank Schmelzer had worked his way up in the financial services industry until, in his early fifties, he was president and CEO of a 240-employee mutual fund organization— a prestigious job, but one that was very stressful. Schmelzer gradually decided that, when he reached the age of fifty-five, he wanted to make a job change; his aim was to leave his job while he still had time to start another career—one with a public-service orientation. Around Schmelzer's fifty-fifth birthday, in 1998, his organization was undergoing a strategic planning and reorganizing process, and as he thought about his goal, Schmelzer decided it was indeed a good time to leave. After quitting his job and then taking some time to explore various options, in early 2000 Schmelzer ended up starting a new job that he really enjoyed: he served as the president and CEO of the Maine Community Foundation, a philanthropic foundation based in Ellsworth, Maine. He held that job until the end of 2008, when, at sixty-five, he retired from it.

> Setting a goal is making an announcement to yourself that you want to do something different. That, in turn, will make it easier to make a change.

Schmelzer did not know what kind of career in public service he might have when he left his mutual fund job, but his goal of leaving cleared the way for him to find his next career. If, on the other hand you already have a specific career change goal in mind, focusing on that goal allows you to work gradually to overcome obstacles. For instance, in the early 1990s, Robyn Michaels had a dream of someday owning a retail store. However, Michaels worked in the nonprofit sector as a social worker and community organizer, so she didn't have a lot of capital to sink into starting a store.

Many people would have kept their dream just that—a dream. But Michaels worked gradually toward her goal. She started reading books from the library about starting a small business. She began buying used store fixtures, such as shelving, when she saw stores going out of business. She saved money toward her goal. She researched her business idea further through a variety of methods, and when Michaels thought she was ready to start her business and had possible concepts in mind, she began gradually looking for a good location with a lease she could afford. As a result of all her waiting and planning, Michaels was able to open a small kitchenware store in 1998—financed with about $35,000 of her own savings, and without going into debt.

identifying the life you want

As important as they are, goals aren't the only tool that can help you think through what you want to accomplish in life. It may be that some of the most important things you want to accomplish aren't a specific

resources

Want more resources to help you think about what you want out of life? Try these:

The Seven Habits of Highly Effective People: Restoring the Character Ethic by Stephen R. Covey (New York: Simon & Schuster, 1989). In Covey's famous book, you'll find an interesting chapter called "Begin with the End in Mind." That chapter includes a section on crafting a mission statement for your life. Doing so can help you think about what you really want in life, and that insight, in turn, can help form the foundation for vocational choices.

Not sure what you want? *Finding Your Own North Star: Claiming the Life You Were Meant to Live* (New York: Three Rivers Press, 2001) by Martha Beck is a very good guide to figuring out what you really want to do.

Does the process of achieving your goals seem daunting? This book will help you with career change goals, but, for good insights on achieving a variety of types of life goals, try *Wishcraft: How to Get What You Really Want* by Barbara Sher with Annie Gottlieb (New York: Ballantine Books, 2004).

For an interesting method for thinking about how your current life does or doesn't correspond to the life you'd like to lead, try reading part of an article that management guru and business author Jim Collins wrote in *Inc.* magazine back in 1997. The entire article is called **"What Comes Next?"** One section is called **"$200 Million and Five Years to Live,"** and that section describes how Collins developed a simple test to determine whether he was on the right track in his life. You can find Collins's writing on that subject in the October 1997 issue of *Inc.*, available online at www.inc.com/magazine/19971001/1335_pagen_5.html.

Alternatively, there is an excellent free audio clip called **"The Self-Employed Professor"** at www.jimcollins.com/audio/biographyA1.mp3. It features Collins describing his own career evolution, including the simple test he came up with for checking his progress in life.

action or achievement; instead, what you want is to live a certain way and embody certain values. Articulating your values—even without a specific action goal attached—can also help you achieve a direction in life you'll be happy with.

Karen and Jim Baroody are examples of the importance of articulating values. In their twenties and early thirties, the Baroodys were both pursuing high-powered careers that involved some long hours—he in the high-tech field of information technology and then the Internet, she at a large financial services firm, ultimately as a senior vice president. But during that period, before they had children, the Baroodys made an unconventional decision: they took a summer off from working and traveled together across country by car. At the time, Jim was changing jobs and was thus in between jobs, and Karen had asked for and gotten a three-month leave of absence from her job to take the trip.

For the Baroodys, that summer traveling was important, because during the trip the couple talked about what really mattered to them in life. "We just spent a lot of time on that trip talking about what was important to us: our family and our quality of life and being able to have a full life—not just work—is more important to us than making huge amounts of money," Karen Baroody recalled. Later, when the couple both made career changes after having children, both of their new career choices reflected, among other things, the value they place on having jobs that allow more time for family. Jim Baroody is now a high school math teacher and department chair in the school district where the Baroodys and their three children live, and Karen Baroody works part-time as a managing director at a nonprofit that helps urban school systems allocate theirs resources more effectively.

what are your life goals?

Stop for a moment. Take a deep breath and think: When did you last sit down and articulate your own goals for your life and values? What do you want to do with the one life you have?

If you have some time now, try the exercises on the following pages. If you don't have uninterrupted time right now—if your boss has just e-mailed you, or if one of your children needs attention, or your lunch break is almost over, or, for any other reason, this isn't a good time to do some contemplation, make an appointment with yourself. Set aside some time in the next week, in a quiet place that you enjoy—wherever that may be—to think about these questions. No matter how busy you are, you deserve to take a little time to think about what's important to *you*.

In the following exercises, let yourself think big. Dream dreams. Talk about what's really important to you. In later chapters, there will be time enough to think about practicalities and finances and mortgage payments and health insurance and so forth. For now, focus on what you want to accomplish in the rest of your life. (Note: If, right now, you don't have any idea what you want to do for work for the rest of your life, don't worry. For this exercise, just focus on things you know you'd like to experience or achieve, in whatever parts of your life that is clear.)

exercise 1: a life well lived

Part A: It's a long time from now. You've recently passed away, at a ripe old age. A local community website is publishing your obituary, and the person who wrote it spoke with your friends, family, and former colleagues before writing a flattering yet accurate description of who you were and how you lived.

Ideally, what will the obituary say? What will friends and family members say about you? What will have been the most noteworthy characteristics of the life you lived? What will people who knew you say about you as a person? And what will be the accomplishments you'll be remembered for?

If you're a writerly type, you could try drafting your own obituary, and see what you come up with. But you can achieve the same effect by just listing points you want the obituary to contain. Try the following questions to guide you:

• What will friends and loved ones say about you?

• What will be the things you're most remembered for?

• What will people say about your work, in retrospect?

Part B: Now look at what you wrote in part A. What does what you've come up with tell you about your goals and values? How, if at all, does this affect your thinking about your career?

exercise 2: the big-time to-do list

Duncan McDougall made his list of things he wanted to do in his life while still quite a young man. But whatever age you are, you can make a list of things you'd like to do over the course of the rest of your life. The items on your list can and should relate to all aspects of your life that are important to you, including work, family, hobbies, fun, and community. And to give yourself credit where credit is due, why not also think back to all the things you've ever wanted to do in life—graduate from high school or college, gain a particular job skill, have a child, you name it—that you've already accomplished?

Part A: Start with the past. Make a list of some of the important goals you've set in the past—from graduating from high school to traveling to a particular destination to starting a family or overcoming any kind of obstacle—that you've achieved. They can be big or small goals. They can be goals whose achievement lots of people saw, or they can be private, personal triumphs. The key thing is that each one was something that was important to you and that you set your mind to and achieved.

Part B: Take a look at your list of accomplishments and next to each item write any skills or resources that particularly helped you accomplish the goal (planning, support from a loved one, hard work, prayer, education, courage, determination, talent, and so on).

Part C: Now think about the rest of the years of your life. What would you really like to do or experience that you haven't already done? Think big. (And think about what *you* want, not what others want for you, or what you think you should want.) What are some things you really want to accomplish before you die?

CHAPTER 3

soul-searching

It's quite possible to change careers successfully without thinking about spirituality or your soul. But if your spiritual life is important to you, then it's natural to think about how it factors into your interest in career change. (For many people, this question isn't part of the equation; if this isn't an issue that interests you or is relevant to you, feel free to skip this chapter.) What's more, some career-changers definitely feel that the sense that they need to change careers comes from someplace deep within them. That's what Lee Finkle Estridge experienced.

For many years, Lee Finkle (who has since married and is now Lee Finkle Estridge) liked her job. She worked as a regional sales rep for a company that sold supplies such as photo albums to professional photographers. Finkle was well known in the photography industry in her region, and she enjoyed her work. Divorced in the 1980s, she worked very hard and for long hours, but the money she earned helped her accomplish a personal goal: ensuring that her daughter could graduate from college without any student loans.

But at some point Finkle started becoming less enthused with her work. Her daughter graduated from college, so that goal was accomplished. As Finkle began contemplating remarriage, she wished she had more time for her personal life than her current job allowed. Those factors were at play in Finkle's life—but she continued to be so busy that it was hard to figure out her next steps.

Then, in 1994, when Finkle was in her mid-forties, she had a moment of epiphany. She had just had surgery and was recuperating but had agreed to give a speech at a photography event in Maine. She and her fiancé were staying at a bed-and-breakfast inn not far from the event. It was a beautiful autumn in New England, and, forced by her operation to slow down, Finkle realized how much she had been missing. The crunch of the leaves underfoot, the beauty of the world around her—such things had been going by in a blur in her too-busy life, she realized. How many autumns, she found herself thinking, have come and gone—and I didn't notice them? And as she thought that, she felt that, in some way, an inner voice from the depths of her soul added something: "And do you want it to be like this for the rest of your life?"

Finkle experienced that moment as the beginning of a wake-up call. It took her a while to make changes in her life after that wake-up call, but she did make changes. In the fall of 1996, Finkle gave notice at the job she'd held for years—without knowing exactly what steps she'd take next, but with a sense that she was going to help people with personal development—a field she'd developed an interest in as a sales rep. After leaving her job, Finkle decided to spend a month and a half on vacation in Maui. While in Maui, Finkle found herself bartering with a personal trainer employed at a hotel spa; in return for training sessions, she offered to coach the personal trainer as he launched his own business. That experience helped Finkle realize she had a natural gift for coaching, and she decided to take training to become a life coach.

Finkle Estridge has now been in practice for years as a certified life coach, and she enjoys a much more balanced lifestyle than in her hectic days in sales. In her old, work-driven lifestyle, she recalled, "I don't think I was fully alive." Now, she said, "I really feel like I'm fully living."

Leaving a job at which you have been successful for years is extremely difficult. In Finkle Estridge's case, though, she felt she had come to a crossroads—and that if she didn't make some kind of changes, she might pay a spiritual and emotional price for it. There are, however, no easy answers or hard-and-fast rules to help you tell the difference between a deep, soul-based desire to change careers and something more superficial. But here are some techniques that may help you as you endeavor to understand what your soul is trying to tell you.

take small steps

You'll notice that Lee Finkle Estridge didn't start off with an immediate insight that said, "Change careers and become a life coach." Instead, the first insight she got was a much smaller step: a recognition that something in her life needed to change so she could have a less hectic lifestyle. Her first step, then, was just realizing that she needed to change—and being willing to start the process of considering that change.

It's often that way with change that comes from some deep place within us: we are given a small step to take—one that may feel hard and scary, but is doable—and if we take that step, the next one becomes apparent. And the next one. And the next one. Soon we will have made major changes in our lives, but ones we could not have foreseen when we started. Richard Nelson Bolles, author of the classic career guide *What Color Is Your Parachute?*, observes in his book's chapter on God, mission, and vocation that we may imagine we will be shown the purpose of our lives from some kind of mountain peak. But instead, Bolles suggests, we are more often guided the way we might be guided by a friend who takes our hand and leads us as we are trying to navigate through a thick fog, in which we can't see anything more than the next step in front of us.[1] In other words, we get a sense of what our next step in life should be, but we can't see beyond that.

> It's often that way with change that comes from some deep place within us: We are given a small step to take—one that may feel hard and scary, but is doable—and if we take that step, the next one becomes apparent.

accept the discomfort of uncertainty

Finkle Estridge suggested that when there's a "pregnant pause" in your life caused by transition, it's good to try to accept the discomfort caused by that uncertainty. "The key is to be okay with discomfort and make friends with it," she said. That, she explained, takes patience, as well as trust in yourself and the universe.

pay attention to significant coincidences

The psychologist Carl Jung used the term *synchronicity* to describe the way life often seems to hand us significant coincidences that have meaning in our lives. Personally, I think of significant coincidences as God's equivalent of the little sticky notes people use to mark interesting passages in books; they are little hints left to alert us to something, usually to help us figure out when we're on the right track.

In his book *Callings: Finding and Leading an Authentic Life*, Gregg Levoy discusses instances of synchronicity and, in particular, their role during significant life transitions. He shares an example from his own career: Levoy, who was a newspaper reporter at the time, was uncertain about the next steps in his career and yet was feeling a need for change. One day, he was driving home while listening to the song "Desperado" by the Eagles. The line in the song that Levoy heard just before getting out of the car mentioned the queen of hearts—and after he opened the car door, he saw a queen of hearts playing card on the curb. Over the next several years, he reports, he found five additional queen cards in odd locations, including, he writes, "a sand dune in Oregon and a mountain wilderness in Colorado." During that period, Levoy eventually came to conclude that he needed more "heart" and intuition in his writing work and in his life.[2]

Such stories of unusual coincidences are more common than you'd think. For example, one summer day in 2007, while visiting relatives,

I was revising a very rough draft of one of the chapters of this book. I took a break to go out walking. As I strolled down a narrow dirt road, I was thinking about the chapter I was working on that day and, in particular, several people mentioned in it. A car approached from the opposite direction; it was traveling very, very slowly, because the road was so narrow. To my surprise, the person driving the car turned out to be one of the people I had just been thinking and writing about as I walked—except that he was several hundred miles from his home and workplace. (He was on vacation, it turned out.) That intense example of synchronicity—which left me with a sense that I certainly seemed to be

---

resources

Let Your Life Speak: Listening for the Voice of Vocation by Parker Palmer (San Francisco: Jossey-Bass, 2000) is a short, thought-provoking book that addresses the topic of discerning your vocation and listening to what your life is trying to tell you. Although he mentions a few Quaker terms such as *clearness committee* and discusses the Quaker phrase "way will open," Palmer generally writes about God in fairly nonsectarian terms. He also shares his own vocational journey.

What Color Is Your Parachute? A Practical Manual for Job-Hunters and Career-Changers (Berkeley, CA: Ten Speed Press, updated annually) by Richard Nelson Bolles includes a helpful chapter on life mission, God, and vocation. In that chapter, Bolles writes from his distinctly Christian perspective but at the same time also acknowledges other religions and encourages non-Christian readers to translate his Christian concepts into their own. The sections of the chapter on receiving guidance one step at a time may be particularly useful to people contemplating career change. The very end of the chapter is likely to be less applicable to many career-changers in today's fast-changing economy, as that section of the chapter seems implicitly to encourage readers to think in terms of having just one true individual work mission in life. (Here's an alternative I'd suggest: career-changers confronting a changing economy or changing life circumstances might instead think in terms of the possibility of having more than one mission over the course of their work lives—or an evolving work mission over time.)

doing the right work at the right time—helped encourage me through the time-consuming process of revising the manuscript.

Have you ever had the experience that you ran into just the right person at just the right time? Not long after Judy Goldberger had first become interested in a possible career change to nursing or midwifery to work with mothers and babies, she happened to run into an acquaintance on a subway train, and the acquaintance happened to be reading a book about childbirth. It turned out that Goldberger's acquaintance was working as an assistant to women in childbirth (often known as a doula), and the program the acquaintance worked for was hiring. That encounter proved a significant coincidence for Goldberger, who ended up working part-time assisting women in childbirth through the same program. Through that job, Goldberger gained experience that helped cement her desire to go to nursing school and then work with mothers and babies as an RN.

If you're curious about this idea of significant coincidences, you might enjoy a book by life coach Cheryl Richardson called *The Unmistakable Touch of Grace* (New York: Free Press, 2005). Richardson calls these kinds of experiences "grace" and writes about her understanding of them in her own life. Levoy's book *Callings* also has a very thoughtful discussion of the subject.

discuss your ideas about career transition with people you trust and respect

In his book *Let Your Life Speak: Listening for the Voice of Vocation*, Parker Palmer, a Quaker and educator, tells a story that beautifully illustrates how, at times, others can help us see things we can't see on our own. Palmer describes how at one point he thought he was going to take a job as president of a school, but first he convened what Quakers call a *clearness committee* to help him think about the decision. In a Quaker clearness committee for an individual facing a decision, a small group sits with the person contemplating the decision. After a period of silent prayer and meditation, group members ask him or her questions. The committee is not designed to come up with an answer to give the individual, but instead to help the individual discover an answer for himself or herself.

One of the people on that particular clearness committee asked Palmer a question that he found surprisingly hard to answer: What would he like most about the job as president? First, Palmer found himself listing a number of things he *wouldn't* like about the job. Finally, Palmer answered that what he would like most was to have his picture in the paper over the word *president*.

Needless to say, Palmer didn't take that job once he realized that that was what appealed to him most about it![3] But had Palmer not stopped to listen, with a little help from his friends, to what his soul was trying to tell him, he might have made a career decision that, despite the prestige it would have granted him, would have not made sense for his life on a deep level. Life is too short to take that kind of risk.

for further reflection

Here is a question to which you may very well not have a ready answer. But it's one you don't have to answer right away. It's simply a question to ponder (and return to periodically) as you contemplate career change. It's this: What is your soul trying to tell you at this time?

CHAPTER 4

gaining perspective

Many people contemplating career change are already working at demanding full-time jobs. You may wonder how, if you have a busy lifestyle and career, you can ever find the time to figure out what your next career move should be.

The problem of determining what kind of work you want to do next is only exacerbated by the wide variety of vocational choices we face today. In many times and places in human history, people often did the same type of work their parents did, or perhaps were apprenticed at an early age to learn a trade. Today, however, there are countless types of jobs and work you could theoretically pursue.

the trouble with too much choice

Ironically, an abundance of choices can make it harder to reach a decision. In his book *The Paradox of Choice: Why More Is Less*, social scientist Barry Schwartz argues that having too many options can actually cause anxiety and dissatisfaction. One reason is that, with many options, it takes more work to make a decision. And when people have more choices, they are likely to be less satisfied with whatever option they do choose—because they remain aware of the benefits of all the alternatives they didn't opt for.[1]

Fortunately, if you are considering a career change, you don't have to research every career option under the sun—nor should you try to. You only have to research a handful of careers that particularly interest you. In fact, you may already have a pretty good idea of what you want to do next, and the challenge is more a matter of getting there than of identifying a goal. But if that's not the case—if, like many potential career-changers, you want or need to change but are not sure what your next move is—here are two options to consider.

option 1: related occupations

Are there occupations closely related to your current career that you might like to pursue? Some career-changers can find inspiration for their next work in their current workplace or industry. Think of the work you have been doing as a room with windows—windows that provide views of a number of related jobs and work settings. Then consider whether any of the career opportunities you can "see" from where you are meet your needs. For example, if you work in a hospital setting and like that setting but not your current job, you may see other jobs in the hospital that you'd like to pursue. Alternatively, you may think of other settings where you could use some of your skills. In career changes to related fields or occupations, the knowledge and experience your current work gives you can help you identify and pursue other, related careers.

Sometimes it's possible to do a new kind of work within an organization you're already in—and thus explore a potential new career direction without changing employers. For example, Gail Snowden spent most of her working life as a banker, working her way up through the ranks of a large bank. But she also made transitions within the bank that, in retrospect, helped prepare her for a later shift into the nonprofit world. At the bank, Snowden moved in 1990 from being a senior credit officer to being president of a then-new inner-city banking initiative. Then, years later, she made further shifts and eventually became president of the bank's own foundation. This gradual shift in the type of work she did—all without leaving her employer—helped Snowden prepare for a later transition into the nonprofit world outside the bank. In addition, during her banking career, Snowden served on a number of nonprofit boards in her spare time, outside of work; that also helped her prepare for a transition to the nonprofit sector. After she left the bank, Snowden served as vice president for finance and operations at a major urban foundation for several years. Then, in her sixties, she went on to become the CEO of Freedom House, a small urban nonprofit that focuses on educational policy and civic engagement.

option 2: getting a different perspective

If, on the other hand, you are considering a more radical career change, ask yourself how you can get a perspective beyond that which your current job provides. If you want to change careers, don't know what you want to do next, and don't see opportunities in your industry, your organization, or fields similar to yours that interest you, you may benefit from seeking out a broader perspective than your current work offers. In particular, if you are thinking of making a career change but not to a field closely related to what you currently do, there's a good chance you will start to figure out your next move while doing something other than the work you do now. New people, projects, or experiences—or just time to yourself—can all help you gain a different point of view and new ideas.

Why is there often a need to get a different perspective before making such a major change? In his classic book *Transitions: Making Sense of Life's Changes*, William Bridges offers some intriguing insights about the nature of handling transition in life, including vocational transitions. He argues that life's transitions tend to follow a natural rhythm of an ending and a letting go of something, followed by a seemingly fallow period—which he calls "the neutral zone"—and then finally culminating in some new beginning, usually in subtle ways.[2] Most life transitions, Bridges notes, are "a slow process."[3]

One implication of this is that the process of changing careers is, like other life transitions, often gradual—and that you will, in many cases, go through a process that involves both emotionally disengaging from your old career and allowing insights about a new career choice to emerge for you. As a result, if you are thinking about making a dramatic change in the type of work you do, reliable inspiration for your next career move is unlikely to strike you while you're, say, frantically gulping down coffee in your cubicle as you struggle to prepare for a big presentation the next day. Any new career ideas that strike you at a moment like that may be overly reactive to current circumstances—"I want to leave all this behind and open up a restaurant on a Caribbean island!" (or raise goats in the country, or whatever other vocational vision of escape appeals to you at that moment)—rather than balanced. In fact, one career counselor who works with senior executives—who, unlike most people, often have the financial cushion not to work for a while—once told me he often encourages many of his clients to take some time off from working if they really want to make changes in their careers. The reason? Executive jobs are so demanding that it's hard for people doing them to think creatively about anything else they may want to do next.

That approach is all well and good for those who have saved enough to afford a considerable stint outside the paid workforce to collect their thoughts. But what about the rest of us? What if you're so busy with your current work—to maintain the cash flow that stems from it—that it's hard to see anything beyond it, yet you know you want change? Here are a variety of ways that you can gain a different perspective on work if you are a potential career-changer.

Time to yourself to think. In 1997, Jim Baroody was working in information technology at an Internet-related start-up. After the birth of his first child that year, Baroody decided to ask if he could reduce his hours to three days a week so he could spend more time at home caring for the baby. (Baroody and his wife both had well-paying jobs.) During that time, while doing things like walking in the woods near his home with his baby, Baroody had some time to think. And he found his perspective in that situation was different than when he was busy in the office. Baroody ultimately decided to leave the business world and instead become a high school teacher, a vocation his father had also pursued.

A period recuperating from an injury or illness. Lee Finkle Estridge (whose story was told in chapter 3) first had the insight that she needed to change her fast-paced work lifestyle while recuperating from surgery. Sometimes either an illness or injury, or the illness or death of a loved one, makes us rethink our priorities—or just gives us time to think about what we really want to do next.

A period of consulting. After leaving a job as an assistant professor at a business school, Ann Gray took on various consulting projects. Consulting introduced her to new people and projects, and, over time, through one of her consulting projects, she met someone who became her business partner; together they bought a business. Thus, the period of consulting ultimately led her to a new phase in her career.

Career counseling or coaching. Jean Kelly was temporarily between jobs as a personal trainer and fitness director in the fitness industry when she saw a notice in a newspaper about a free career-counseling class being offered at a nearby library. By taking the class, Kelly had a chance to think about what she'd liked and disliked about various jobs, to take career-related tests, and to discuss the results with a career counselor. And, based in large part on the insights of the career counselor, Kelly ended up pursuing a new career as a chiropractor, an occupation she enjoys today.

A break afforded by an early-retirement or buyout offer, or a good severance payment. Sometimes organizations that need to downsize offer longtime employees an incentive to quit, such as some combination of financial support and benefits. (Alternatively, employees with considerable tenure who get laid off may receive a severance payment that provides a bit of a cushion.) Buyout offers, which may involve a lump-sum payment or payments over time, can give the people who take them a bit of time to figure out their next career moves. Although it's important not to stagnate or withdraw from the world during such a transition period, people who have worked for a long time at one organization can sometimes benefit from having a little time to figure out how they want to reinvent themselves.

Nick Pappas had the opportunity for that kind of reinvention. He had worked for twenty-seven years at a high-tech company that had grown to be, at the time, one of the world's largest. But when the industry changed and his employer began downsizing, Pappas opted for a "transition assistance" package that was offered to longtime employees. After leaving the company in June 1994, Pappas spent that summer painting his house as well as taking advantage of some outplacement services offered by his former employer. In the fall, Pappas began seriously exploring ideas for his next step: he was interested in starting or buying a small business. After a period of research and exploration, in 1995 Pappas started Lizzy's Ice Cream, a retail business he has now run for more than a decade.

Anything you enjoy doing in your spare time, away from work. In truth, virtually any activity you do could theoretically lead you in the direction of a new type of work—particularly if you have already decided that you want change and are thus especially open to new possibilities. For example, Judy Goldberger (introduced in chapter 3) had already decided that at some point she was going to leave her job doing fundraising for a small nonprofit when, in 2000, a pregnant friend asked Goldberger to be present when the friend gave birth. When she attended that birth, Goldberger was struck with "the miracle of the moment" of birth, and as she watched the nurse-midwives she found herself thinking she might like similar work. After research to learn about her options, several years of part-time work assisting in labor and delivery, and a return to school, Goldberger became a nurse who works with mothers and babies in the postpartum unit of a hospital.

Another example of finding a new career direction unexpectedly: George Watts, a former director of finance for Canada's Conservative Party, was working at a government job in Canada but felt ready for a change. Watts ended up in a new career as an innkeeper—after he stopped at a bed-and-breakfast inn, the Moses Nickerson House on Cape Cod in Massachusetts, while traveling. There he fell in love with (and later married) the innkeeper.

Work that exposes you to different kinds of people and opportunities. Although some people gain perspective by finding some time to themselves, it is also possible to get insights into very different new career directions even when you're frantically busy. But it helps if some of the things that make you so busy are different from your current career. Consider the case of Lois Ford and Lou Ciercielli, a married couple who are both engineers and were working as engineer-managers for a *Fortune* 500 company. The couple feared that the plant where they were working would be closed (it later was, in fact), so they hatched a backup plan. While still working at their full-time managerial jobs, they bought a beautiful old house in a rural town not too far away and turned it into a bed-and-breakfast inn, which they ran on the weekends.

Not surprisingly, this decision made the couple's life extremely busy—too busy, they say, in retrospect—for several years. But one component

resources

Transitions: Making Sense of Life's Changes by William Bridges, second edition (Cambridge, MA: Perseus Books, 2004). This is a wonderful, classic book about understanding times of transition in your life.

Downshifting: How to Work Less and Enjoy Life More by John D. Drake (San Francisco: Berrett-Koehler, 2000). A former CEO of a large human resources consulting firm, Drake wrote this practical book for people seeking a way to lead a less hectic, less work-dominated life.

If, in this chapter, you find yourself intrigued by the stories of Gail Snowden or Elaine Cummings—who both made career changes that involved more than one step—be sure to take a look at *What Color Is Your Parachute? A Practical Manual for Job-Hunters and Career-Changers* by Richard Nelson Bolles (Berkeley, CA: Ten Speed Press, updated annually). This classic career book has lots of great resources and insights appropriate for career-changers. In particular, there's a handy section in recent editions that discusses the benefits of making career changes in two stages rather than one (and illustrates that process with a chart); it's a section definitely worth reading by any potential career-changer. Exact page numbers may vary (depending on which year's edition of the book you have), but in the 2008 edition the section and chart are on pages 166 and 167.

of their busyness—their bed-and-breakfast—was also exposing Ford and Ciercielli to new ideas. For one thing, Ford recalled, the bed-and-breakfast guests were an interesting lot, some of whom had intriguing or varied careers. Meeting the guests and talking to them, Ford thinks, was very encouraging to the couple as they began considering career alternatives beyond the corporate sphere. As it turned out, the fact that guests liked the homemade cookies Ford baked and wanted to order them as gifts ultimately gave Ford and Ciercielli the seed of an idea for their next business: a bakery that makes items such as cookies and award-winning brownies. Today, Ford and Ciercielli have long since stopped running the bed-and-breakfast, and both of them had left the *Fortune* 500 company by the time the plant where they had worked was closed. Together, they run the Bellows House Bakery in Walpole, New Hampshire.

A period trying out a different job or jobs. It is even possible to seek out work simply because it will expose you to new perspectives. Before her children were born, Elaine Cummings had been a teacher in a public high school, teaching business education classes like shorthand and typing. When she returned to the paid workforce in the mid-1980s, Cummings wanted to try something different, but she wasn't sure what. So she used her secretarial skills to apply for and get secretarial jobs in industries in which she thought she might be interested in pursuing a career—as a way of exploring the industries and gaining perspective on them, while earning her living. First Cummings worked in a law office—but she decided legal work was too much about arguments and conflict. Then she worked as a secretary in the advertising industry—but she felt advertising was a little too superficial. Finally, she found a job as an editorial assistant at a magazine—and there discovered an industry she liked and wanted to join. Once on staff at the magazine, Cummings was able to identify a career path that appealed to her and start to map out steps toward her new goal. She subsequently became a managing editor at a magazine and later an editor at a large consulting firm.

getting beyond the familiar

Different as all these stories are, many have one thing in common: *they involve people who gained insights that helped them make a substantial career change while doing something other than the work they had been doing before.* It was only when they got outside the demands of the job environment they had been in, and were exposed to other influences, that they could start to envision what other work setting they might want to join. Only when these individuals were outside the familiar could they start to discern a new direction.

for further reflection

- Are there occupations closely related to your current career that you might like to pursue? Write down any ideas that occur to you. Now ask yourself how you can use your current work, your network of work contacts, or your industry knowledge to find out more about those occupations.

- If, on the other hand, you think you may want to pursue a more radical career change, how can you start to make space to get a new perspective on your life? Can you think of a low-risk way to start to get out of your everyday routine and get new perspectives on your life and work? Maybe it's something as simple as making time every morning to write in a journal—or taking a quiet, restful vacation that gives you time to think. Or maybe you want to give up some existing leisure activities or habits that feel like they've outlived their usefulness, to give yourself more time to think, relax, and explore new directions. What feels right?

career change and your personal life

When you first made career choices—when you chose the type of work, training, or education you pursued as a young adult just entering the workforce—your family and life situation may have been very different from the way it is today. At the time, you might never have imagined the life you lead now. In fact, later stages of life may not have been much on your mind at all when you were first choosing a career as a young adult.

For people contemplating career change after they've been in the workforce, it's a little different. Whatever your family situation or stage of life—single, married with children, married without children, divorced, retired from a first career, you name it—your current life situation will factor into the type of career change you make and the way you make the transition. What's more, changing personal circumstances—such as the birth of children, children growing up, divorce, or getting older—can contribute to the decision to change careers as well as affect the kind of career change a person makes. In fact, that's not uncommon. At the end of this chapter, you'll find an exercise that will help you think through the circumstances in your own personal life that may affect your own decisions about career choice.

The good news is that, these days, it may be a little easier to fit career change in with the rest of your life. Although there are many, many disadvantages to today's fast-changing economy, one positive aspect of it is that, because career change has been forced on so many people by economic circumstances (such as downsizing and shifts in the economy), career change has become more socially acceptable. That may make it a little more feasible to forge a new work solution that will work for you, your loved ones, and the rest of your personal life. The increased prevalence of two-career couples over the past generation or two has also made career change feasible for more families: if both spouses have paid jobs outside the home, it may be easier to weather any period of reduced earnings (whether transitional or long-term) that may accompany a career change.

if you're married

However, if you're married or otherwise in a long-term committed relationship, your partner may not be enthusiastic about your interest in changing careers. William Bridges, author of the classic book *Transitions: Making Sense of Life's Changes*, observes that a spouse may feel panic when his or her partner changes—and family members often unconsciously resist changes to the family system.[1] In a similar vein, Herminia Ibarra writes in her excellent book *Working Identity: Unconventional Strategies for Reinventing Your Career* that those close to us expect us to stay the same and that "most people who have made big career changes have heard loved ones tell them 'You're out of your mind.'"[2]

But in her book, Ibarra, a business school professor, focused on well-educated professionals who started off in careers like business, law, academia, and medicine—and who were mostly in their late thirties and early forties when changing careers.[3] It may be more likely that such a career change—leaving behind a well-paying professional job in midcareer when the career may have involved a big investment in specialized training and education—will be questioned by those close to the career-changer. The group of people I interviewed came from a somewhat broader range of backgrounds; it included people who sought more training to change careers to a job with better pay or benefits, people who were changing careers in their mid-fifties, and people who changed careers after a layoff.

At any rate, I found a somewhat different pattern from what Ibarra found. When, in the course of writing a newspaper series on career change, I interviewed people whose spouse had changed careers and they described their reactions to their partner's career change plans, those reactions were all over the map—from horror to excitement. Many of the married people I interviewed who had changed careers had spouses who appeared to be at least moderately supportive—and in some cases, quite supportive—of the career change. Holly Gandolfo, for example, is a nurse who used to work in sales and customer service for an airline but dreamed of entering nursing. She said that her husband was really supportive of her career change goal; in fact, he urged her to pursue the nursing degree. At one point, as she recalled, he told her: "I've heard a lot about this [goal of becoming a nurse], but I don't see you doing anything about it."

> A spouse these days is less likely to feel that his or her partner is jeopardizing a job that could last for decades by changing careers, and, in fact, layoffs are the catalyst for some career changes.

If, in general, some spouses today are more willing to support or even encourage career change, that may be a reflection of a number of factors. One is the uncertainty of the contemporary economy; a spouse these days is less likely to feel that his or her partner is jeopardizing a job that could last for decades by changing careers, and, in fact, layoffs are the catalyst for some career changes. Greater spousal support for career change could also reflect the fact that, in an era in which it's common for women to work outside the home, some families may have a little more flexibility to manage a career transition, as one spouse may be able to subsidize the other's career change. Also, a spouse may in some cases perceive that a partner's new career might benefit the couple's family in some way, such as higher earnings or more family-friendly working conditions.

On the other hand, the fact that many of the successful career-changers I interviewed who were married had reasonable spousal support for their career change may mean something different: it may simply mean that, if you're married, you are more likely to be successful in changing careers if your spouse thinks it's a good idea! Career change can definitely challenge a marriage (and has been known to coincide with or be followed by divorce), and it's important to find out how your spouse really feels about your ideas. It's important to talk with him or her about your thoughts on career change, and find out your partner's thoughts and feelings—and insights—about the topic.

> It's important to talk with your partner about your thoughts on career change, and find out your partner's thoughts and feelings—and insights—about the topic.

And, no matter what your spouse's initial reaction is, it may change over time. Although successful career change can offer emotional or financial benefits in the long run, the process of career transition is often stressful not only for the person changing careers but also for his or her partner. Many issues can come up for spouses, including:

- Feeling uncertainty during a transition
- Having financial concerns related to reduced household income
- Not feeling sufficiently included in the career-change decision
- Juggling time demands and childcare
- Watching a partner go through emotional ups and downs

On the other hand, on the plus side, spouses may take pleasure in a partner's new accomplishments. For instance, Karen Baroody said that when her husband Jim was changing careers to go into teaching, "it was actually kind of fun for me because it was so exciting for him."

When spouses indicated that they found some aspect of their partner's career change process challenging, it was often for very practical reasons, such as reduced income or financial uncertainty. A spouse may also sometimes have mixed feelings if the career-changing partner has been staying at home with children and decides to go back into the paid workforce (a move that is in itself a major career transition, and one that is often accompanied by career change). In this situation, too, spousal reactions can vary substantially. Carol Fishman Cohen and Vivian Steir Rabin, authors of a book called *Back on the Career Track: A Guide for Stay-at-Home Moms Who Want to Return to Work*, advise their readership of stay-at-home mothers that a husband's response when his wife decides to resume a career outside the home can range from "thrilled" to "far less supportive."[4]

when your spouse is skeptical

What if you're married and your spouse is not enthusiastic about your career change idea—and you want to pursue it anyway? That's definitely an issue that some couples face. Every couple's situation is different, but here's how one career-changer, Lindsay Frucci, reported that she and her husband weathered that challenge. Frucci had an idea for a product—fat-free brownies—and wanted to start a small business rather than continue to earn money the way she had been, selling real estate. He wasn't enthusiastic. The Fruccis' solution? They compromised. Lindsay Frucci said she and her husband agreed that she would take her product idea to the local office of SCORE (www.score.org), a nonprofit that is affiliated with the U.S. Small Business Administration and that offers free counseling to people who want to start businesses. If the businesspeople at SCORE who evaluated her idea thought it wasn't a good one, she'd drop it. As it turned out, Lindsay Frucci found experts at SCORE who liked her product and helped her refine her business concept, and she did indeed launch the business, No Pudge! Foods Inc. However, given her husband's initial skepticism, Lindsay Frucci continued to sell real estate for a while and used her real estate earnings to finance the initial launch of her start-up business, rather than relying more heavily on the rest of the couple's financial resources during that period.

That particular story ended happily. The nonfat brownie mix business that Lindsay Frucci started grew and eventually was sold, and the sale of the company contributed significantly to the couple's financial well-being. But many small businesses *don't* succeed. By having outside experts evaluate the idea up front and then limiting the potential impact of the initial launch of the business on the family's finances, the Fruccis wisely hedged their bets a bit.

if you're single

People who are not married and have no children face a very different set of career-change challenges than people who are married. On the one hand, if you're single, have no children at home, and live alone, you can make decisions on your own; no one is likely to complain if you decide to work until midnight or plow all your discretionary income into a new career direction. On the other hand, single people usually have to finance career change out of their own savings and cash flow, or with loans—because, unless they're independently wealthy, there's no one else to help pay the bills. That can make managing a career transition more challenging. What's more, people who are single, divorced, or widowed parents and are raising young children face particular challenges in changing careers, because single parents often face time and money constraints simultaneously.

> One strategy—perhaps especially appropriate for people without children at home—is a two-career solution, in which you start launching one career or training for it part-time while still working in your initial career.

For single people, career changes that can be accomplished without a substantial reduction in earnings—such as a modest change to a different industry or work setting that can be achieved using transferable skills or knowledge, or a career change that is accomplished in stages over time—may be worth exploring. It also helps if you're able to be thrifty and save money while at your current job. One strategy—

perhaps especially appropriate for people without children at home—is a two-career solution, in which you start launching one career or training for it part-time while still working in your initial career. (See chapter 14 for more information about this approach.) And if you're returning to school and incurring debt in the process, it's important to first do enough independent research into your career prospects to be truly confident in your ability to pay the debt back with earnings from your new career.

The bottom line? The circumstances of your personal life will play a role in your decision to change careers, the way you choose to manage the career transition, and the new career you choose. Taking some time to think through the relevant issues and discuss them with people close to you can pay big dividends in the future.

resources

Transitions: Making Sense of Life's Changes, second edition, by William Bridges (Cambridge, MA: Da Capo Press, 2004). Although it was first written more than twenty-five years ago (and subsequently revised), this classic book on life transitions offers plenty of timeless wisdom about the emotional aspects of adjusting to life change. The chapter on the effect of transitions on relationships presents interesting insights and is important reading.

If you are a stay-at-home parent contemplating career change as part of a transition back to the paid labor force, that can be a particularly daunting transition. It's also one in which family obligations loom particularly large. Carol Fishman Cohen and Vivian Steir Rabin, two Harvard Business School grads who became stay-at-home moms and then returned to the paid workforce, have written an excellent book called ***Back on the Career Track: A Guide for Stay-at-Home Moms Who Want to Return to Work*** (New York: Warner Business Books, 2007). The book focuses a lot on highly educated professional women, and some mothers may find that off-putting; on the whole, though, *Back on the Career Track* has loads of practical information for stay-at-home parents in career transition. It includes a chapter specifically on managing family and household issues related to returning to the paid workforce.

support comes in many forms

Changing careers is hard work, and it helps to have emotional support when you get discouraged or scared. You don't, however, have to rely just on those closest to you for emotional support during career change. Although your friends and family are obvious choices to turn to, there may be additional sources of emotional support, as well. Here are some possibilities to consider:

- **Fellow career-changers.** You may find one potential source of support in other people who are in the middle of the same career change you are seeking to make. This is most applicable to career-changers going through some kind of schooling or formal training; in such cases, you might make a friend who is also changing into the same career you are, or you might form a study group with other students.

- **People in the industry you want to join.** If you've identified an industry that interests you, involving yourself in industry associations, conferences, or events can prove indirect support for career change—in that, by interacting with people in the field you want to join, you can gain valuable information, contacts, and industry insights that can help you launch your new career. More subtly, your interactions with people doing the kind of work you want to do can make your dream and goal more real to you.

- **Career counselors or career coaches.** For some career-changers, the perspective of a professional can be very helpful. One caveat, however: if you are considering working with a career counselor or coach, be aware that, although there are many excellent career counselors and career coaches, there are also some not-so-great ones. If you have never worked with a career counselor or coach before, it's important to acquaint yourself with some of the potential pitfalls. *What Color Is Your Parachute?* by Richard

Nelson Bolles has an excellent appendix on choosing career counselors that should be required reading before hiring a career counselor. That appendix discusses both questions to ask a counselor before you hire him or her, and what to avoid.

- **Outplacement seminars, classes, or counseling, if offered by a former employer.** Generally, if you are laid off or are taking some kind of voluntary buyout offer, and free outplacement counseling is offered as part of the severance package, it is at least worth exploring. Middle or upper managers often tend to receive more extensive outplacement services from their former employers than lower-level employees do.

- **Mentors.** Sometimes career-changers are able to form a mentoring relationship with someone who has achieved a type of career or career goal they are trying to accomplish. Such relationships can be very valuable.

for further reflection

Read through the following list of some of the ways in which life circumstances can affect career-change decisions. Do any of them apply to you? Write down all those that apply—as well as any others that occur to you—in your career change journal.

- I am financially responsible, either solely or with my spouse, for children or college students.

- As I get older, I find the work I used to do too draining or physically demanding—or I think I will in the future.

- My spouse and I are starting a family or have started one, and I want to earn more to support our family.

- Now that I have children, I need more flexibility in my schedule to take care of them.

- I have caregiving responsibilities for ill family members or older relatives, so I need scheduling flexibility.

- As I get older, I am more focused on finding meaning in my work. I want to use the time I have left in the workforce to do work that matters to me.

- I can't do the work I used to do because of an injury or medical condition.

- I am single, and any career change I make has to be something I can finance out of my own income and savings—or from loans that I am extremely confident I can repay.

- My kids have grown up—and now that household expenses are lower, I can afford to change careers to something I've been wanting to do.

- I don't have children to support.

- My spouse's job could provide us with benefits such as health insurance, if need be.

- My work is the only source of benefits such as health insurance for me and/or my household.

- Now that I am divorced, I need to earn more.

- My children are approaching college age, and I want to earn more.

- I earned enough in my previous career/first career that now that I'm older, I can do something I really enjoy—even if it doesn't pay as much.

- My spouse and I both work full-time and have children, and we're extremely busy all the time; I'd prefer to work less than full-time or have scheduling flexibility, so that our family life wouldn't be so stressed.

- I am getting older and I want to make a career change while I still have time, energy, and my health.

- I stopped working outside the home when I had children. Now that they are older, I want to go back into the paid workforce.

- I have retired and want to do something different from my previous career, perhaps on a less than full-time basis.

- If necessary when I make a career change, our household could get by for a while by relying on my spouse's income during my transition.

(continued)

(continued)

- When my children were little, I reduced my career-related ambitions so that I could spend more time caring for them. Now that they're growing up, I have more flexibility, and I'd like to make changes in the kind of work I do.

Add any additional statements that come to mind.

Now look over what you've written. What does your list tell you about factors in your personal life that you should consider in your career change? What are some features that, based on these factors, you want in your next career? Write down any phrase or phrases that describes those features; the phrases could range from "personal fulfillment" to "health insurance," depending on your life circumstances.

Next, what does your list tell you about any features you *don't* want your next career to include? These could range from "seventy-hour work weeks" to "low wages." Write those features down, too.

If you are in a long-term relationship, how do you think your career change plans could affect your partner? Think about issues ranging from the emotional (fear of uncertainty) to the practical (concerns about time, household chores, and money). Can you talk to him or her about your goals and dreams, the changes you might go through, the type of support you will need, and how he or she might be affected?

If you're not in a long-term relationship, who close to you may be affected by your career change plans? Whom can you ask for support?

the question of money— and health insurance

Many people perceive money as a major obstacle to making a significant change in their careers. So if you feel trapped in your current work by the financial obligations of adult life, you're not alone. But with some determination and creative thinking, you may be able to find a way to make a career change that suits your life *and* your financial responsibilities.

Consider the story of Tommy Vaudo. Vaudo didn't grow up with the kind of financial advantages that would have made it easy for him to go to college right after graduating from high school. When Tommy Vaudo was about ten or eleven, his father died, and Vaudo said he and his brothers and sisters ended up in foster care. After Vaudo graduated from high school in 1980, he joined the Navy. Once finished with his military service, he worked in an automotive center and then at a meat market, but he didn't like either job particularly well. So he got into a construction-related union, the laborers' union. In that job, Vaudo often worked removing asbestos. Working around asbestos, even with appropriate equipment, wasn't exactly Vaudo's dream job—but the pay was comparatively good. "You do whatever you have to do," he explained. He also worked with a friend, installing and maintaining swimming pools.

But Vaudo dreamt of getting more education. "I kept saying, 'I want to go back to college,'" he recalled. He had an interest in working in a medical field. As a child, he had admired the respect that his aunt, a nurse, got in her work, and he liked the job she did. He remembered at one point working in a medical area while on a job with the laborers' union, watching the doctors and nurses and wanting to be one of them.

The event that led Vaudo to seriously pursue further education was the death of one of his sisters, at a young age, of cancer. He recalled that, when his sister was dying, she told him she regretted never having pursued her dreams in life—and she observed that he hadn't done what he wanted to do in life, either. That got Vaudo thinking for a while about his own dream of getting more education to start a new career. He remembered thinking to himself, "She's right. Why aren't I doing what I want to do?"

One day in 1995, Vaudo, who by then was in his thirties, went down to the local community college and inquired about taking courses. He enrolled, ultimately transferring from the community college to a local branch of his state university so he could get a bachelor's degree in nursing. In 2001, he graduated from college with his bachelor's degree, at the age of thirty-eight.

Today, Vaudo is a nurse—one of America's most in-demand professions, although often a highly stressful one. Vaudo now makes a better salary than before he went back to school, and he finds that working with people suits him better than his previous occupations did. In addition to his nursing job, he is currently also going to law school—pursuing another career dream of his.

Although Vaudo now makes more money than he did before becoming a nurse, he couldn't have changed careers into nursing without some financial flexibility. In his case, he went to college while working. But Vaudo couldn't manage that schedule without changing jobs, because he needed a job that had a lot of weekend hours, when he wasn't in class. So while going to college Vaudo worked as a limousine driver. That gave him the weekend hours he needed—and he could study while sitting in his limo at the airport, waiting to pick up a ride.

However, being a limo driver meant taking a substantial pay cut—from the more than $19 an hour, plus overtime, he had made as a laborer, to $10 to $12 an hour, including tips.

How did the Vaudos manage through that period when Tommy Vaudo was earning less? They spent less. Tommy Vaudo said he and his wife and child talked about how his going back to school would mean a change in their lifestyle for a number of years. During that period, the Vaudos, a two-income family, wouldn't be eating out at restaurants as much, ordering as much take-out food, or going on family vacations to Florida. And they wouldn't be buying a new car during the time he was in school, either. But, he reasoned, the Vaudos' favorite vacation spot wouldn't close because the family didn't go there during those years—and their favorite steakhouse would still be there when he graduated, too. "We set the plan and then we stuck to it," he said.

It may not sound like fun, but Tommy Vaudo's story illustrates something that's true for many career-changers: even if, in changing careers, you may ultimately improve your earnings, you sometimes have to go through a transition in which you have less disposable income. (Not always, by any means, but often.) There are several reasons this may be true. For one thing, you sometimes need more training or education, as Vaudo did, to enter a new field. You may have to spend money for the additional training, or, if you get training on the job, you may earn less while developing your new skills and gaining experience. Finally, if you start a business of your own, it may well take time to grow revenues. As a result, a career change—even between two fields that offer roughly similar earnings potential over the long term—can often mean taking a pay cut in the short term. That isn't always so, however—and the less radical your career change, the more likely you are to be able to transfer skills and earning power early on in your transition. (Also, the less you're earning now, the easier it may be to replicate your current earnings.)

> Even if, in changing careers, you may ultimately improve your earnings, you sometimes have to go through a transition in which you have less disposable income.

Let's break the money questions that surround career change down into two parts—because there really are two separate issues. One question is the issue of how much you need to make long-term. The other, shorter-term question is your financial flexibility and ability to manage any costs associated with making a career change (such as education costs, start-up costs if you're starting a small business, or possibly lower earnings while transitioning into a new field). We'll examine the big-picture financial issue first.

your long-term financial needs

Not surprisingly, money and financial needs play a big role in most career change considerations—but it's not always the same role. Which of the following five financial scenarios sound like they may fit your situation?

Scenario 1: Changing careers to earn more (or get better benefits). This is a common type of career change, particularly among relatively young people and people whose current career isn't ideal in terms of either pay or benefits, or both.

Scenario 2: Changing careers to earn about the same—but be happier. Some career-changers end up changing to a field in which compensation isn't markedly different from that in their previous field—but the new job just suits them better, or they want a change.

Scenario 3: Changing careers when you are willing to take a modest pay cut in order to have greater satisfaction or do a certain type of work. There are many people who are willing to earn a bit less if it means they can be in a job or environment they'd prefer.

Scenario 4: Changing careers when you are willing to take a significant pay cut in return for greater satisfaction. Sometimes people are willing to take a substantial pay cut for lifestyle or job satisfaction reasons. This type of career change is seen among some parents, often mothers, who are caring for young children and are willing to give up substantial pay for greater scheduling flexibility. It's also found among people who leave high-paying but high-pressure jobs for some type of significant lifestyle change. Finally, it's sometimes seen among older workers who retire successfully from one career and start another career later in life.

Scenario 5: Changing careers because circumstances are forcing you to, because of conditions in your industry or a change in your personal circumstances. This may mean accepting a pay cut. The first four scenarios may be moot. If it's become difficult to find a job like one you've had in the past because of industry changes or an economic downturn, or you are injured in a way that requires you to change the kind of work you do, or your circumstances change otherwise in ways that force you to change careers, you may need to change careers without necessarily either being happier than you were in your old job *or* making more money. In such a situation—which is unfortunately not unusual in today's turbulent economy—you may, for a while, just need to make the best you can of a difficult situation. But you can also be planning ways to regroup, so that you can eventually find work that meets more of your goals.

All five scenarios represent perfectly legitimate points of view, and there are career-changers of all five types. What's important, though, is that you have a solid understanding of what would work for you— and keep that in mind as you evaluate potential new careers. This is particularly true if you are thinking of pursuing a type of career change that may not be lucrative, such as a change to some type of field in the arts. Sometimes, when people attempt an ideals-driven career change to something they'd really love to do, they may find after a while that, financially, the numbers just don't work for them—and they can't make the kind of living they require in the new field. Sometimes, too, career-changers invest in additional training or education in the hopes that it will lead to a better-paying job—and then can't find such a job or are disappointed in the earnings they receive in the new career.

You can lower the risk of either kind of disappointment by doing some research and thinking up front. Use the questions and resources in this chapter to think seriously about your own financial goals and needs—

before you begin to research several possible career options. (We'll talk further about that research process in part II of this book.) Thinking seriously about your own financial needs, then learning more about the fields you're interested in, are great steps that can help you anchor your career dreams in reality—and increase your odds of successful career change.

financing a transition period

Then there's the second money question related to career change: financing a transition. Career change sometimes means a transition that entails lost or lower wages. Even people who expect eventually to make more in their new career may face a transitional drop in income or a transitional increase in expenses. How do successful career-changers manage such transition periods? Here are seven factors that can make it easier. Any one of them can help, and a combination of several is even better.

Savings. Some people set aside some of what they earn in their first career to form a financial cushion when they change careers. Karen and Jim Baroody, who both changed careers from the business world to, respectively, working in a nonprofit and teaching high school, lived well below their means when they were working at well-paying jobs in business. "We always wanted to be saving," Karen Baroody recalled.

---

resources

Do you think a career change you want to make might entail a period of greater frugality? If you're interested in exploring the idea of spending less so you can achieve more of your goals, there are any number of guides to frugal living.

One good one is *America's Cheapest Family Gets You Right On the Money: Your Guide to Living Better, Spending Less, and Cashing In on Your Dreams* by Steve and Annette Economides (New York: Three Rivers Press, 2007). The Economides write with a warm, inviting tone and offer lots of good money-saving ideas.

Frugal Living for Dummies by Deborah Taylor-Hough (Indianapolis, IN: Wiley, 2003) also contains many useful tips.

As a result of the Baroodys' savings—and Karen Baroody's income at the time—Jim Baroody was able to return to graduate school to earn a one-year master's degree in education, without incurring debt. Then, after Jim Baroody started teaching and the couple's third child was born, Karen Baroody was able to stay home full-time and then part-time with the couple's young children.

Spouse's earnings. Some career-changers are able to manage their career change because their spouse provides benefits and enough income to pay many of the family's bills for a period of time—particularly if the family cuts back on discretionary expenses like vacations. In some cases, a couple may make career transitions in tandem to better facilitate a career change. For example, one spouse may change his or her working arrangements to have benefits or better hours—in order to make the other's career change more feasible.

Severance. Sometimes companies that are seeking to shrink their workforces will offer "buyout" financial incentives to longtime employees who are willing to leave the company. Other companies offer long-time employees who are laid off significant severance, equivalent to a number of months of pay. Either type of package can make it easier for people to change careers, because it gives them more time and resources to prepare for a new field.

Frugality. A number of the successful career-changers I interviewed were either naturally frugal or became so when confronted with a career change they really wanted to make. For example, Duncan McDougall, who changed careers from management consulting to starting a non-profit, was naturally fairly thrifty. He tended to save at least half his salary while working as a management consultant. McDougall's savings and frugal spending habits doubtless made it easier for him to make a transition to starting a nonprofit, the Children's Literacy Foundation.

Giving up free time. It's possible to change careers by working two jobs at once—at least for a while. When Robyn Michaels opened her kitchenware store—a longtime dream of hers—for about eight months she continued to work half-time in her job as a community organizer for a nonprofit. (Michaels had a good relationship with her boss, who

How do career-changers who need to spend less, save more, or bring in more income finance a career transition? In addition to loans and savings, here are some of the methods some career-changers said they used. This list is based on comments from and observations about more than a dozen different career-changers. (Note: You don't have to use all of these methods! In fact, no single individual mentioned using all of them; most mentioned one or a few.)

- Eat out less.

- Cut back on vacation spending and travel.

- Keep your car longer before you buy a new one.

- When you buy your next car, get a less expensive one.

- Buy a used car.

- If you happen to live in a city that has good public transportation, do without a car. In cities with good public transportation, this isn't necessarily as hard to do as it sounds. In some cities there are now even car-sharing services, such as Zipcar (www .zipcar.com); members of a car-sharing service can rent cars by the hour, when needed.

- (For renters) Share housing with roommates.

- (For homeowners) Rent out a room.

- Have a relative who is willing to share household expenses move in with you.

- Move to a smaller or less expensive living space.

- Stop buying coffee and soda on the go, outside the home.

- Moonlight, doing extra work in your spare time while saving to make a career transition.

- Get financial help from relatives.

- Examine family cell phone spending.

- Shop at thrift stores or yard sales.

- Switch to a less expensive cable TV package.

- Do without cable TV entirely.

> - Live below your means; if you currently have a well-paying job, save rather than letting your expenses grow to match your income.
> - Take books out of the library rather than buying them.
> - If you plan to pay for your children's college education, consider sending them to a state university rather than a private one.
> - If you are starting a small business, buy used furniture or fixtures.

was willing to allow her flexible scheduling.) It's also possible, as Vaudo's story illustrates, to work while going to school.

Going slower. Often you can substitute time for money—in that, if you can't afford to make a career change quickly, you may be able to make it more gradually. For example, if you don't have the financial flexibility to go to school full-time, maybe you can go to school part-time while still working full-time. Or maybe you can start now to prepare gradually for a career change that you may make later in life, at a time more conducive for it.

Government programs. Are you changing careers because you've been laid off, due to industry changes that will make it hard to find another similar job? If so, it's worth checking to see what programs are available in your state or local area to help dislocated workers. For instance, as of this writing, the state of Michigan is sponsoring a program called "No Worker Left Behind" that offers eligible displaced workers in Michigan funds for retraining if they pursue certain kinds of new career paths, such as training for high-growth occupations.[1]

managing the health insurance challenge

If you live in the United States, you have to think about more than salary when changing careers; in the fragmented (and confusing) U.S. health insurance system, maintaining health insurance during a career transition can be daunting.

There are, however, a variety of alternatives that career-changers can explore for maintaining health coverage during a career transition.

If you are married, one of the best options is to obtain good health coverage through your spouse's job. Another option is, of course, getting good health insurance at a new job you take—or, if you have health insurance at your current job, continuing to work at the job enough hours to maintain coverage during a transition. Yet another alternative you should be aware of is the Consolidated Omnibus Budget Reconciliation Act (COBRA), a federal law that helps many workers to maintain their coverage through their employer's group health insurance during transitions of up to eighteen months after leaving a job. (*Caution:* Even with coverage under COBRA, you will generally have to pay the COBRA premiums yourself, so be sure to find out at least approximately what they will cost *before* you take the plunge.) Another piece of federal legislation, the Health Insurance Portability and Accountability Act of 1996 (HIPAA), may make it easier to transfer your coverage from one group plan to another, or to obtain individual coverage when leaving a group plan. If you are attending a college or university program while retraining, know that some schools offer some type of insurance plan, at the student's expense; check with your school to find out if this is the case, and what the plan does and doesn't cover. Also, associations, such as professional or business associations, sometimes offer health plans that their members can purchase.

The alternative to coverage through some type of group is the individual health insurance market. Unfortunately, state regulations on health insurance vary widely, so it's difficult to make general statements about individual insurance in the United States. In one state, private-sector insurance companies may not be allowed to charge more to people with a serious medical condition or to refuse to sell insurance to them, but in another state that may be perfectly legal. In other words, when it comes to health insurance options for individuals purchasing their own insurance, a lot depends on location.

One source of information: You can do an Internet search for your state's insurance department. Also, many states offer high-risk pools for health insurance for people seeking individual health insurance but unable to qualify for it in the commercial market; the National Association of State Comprehensive Health Insurance Plans has a list of links to state risk pools on its website, www.naschip.org.

transitioning smoothly

You don't necessarily have to weather a transitional or preparatory period when you make a significant change in your career. Generally, the more you can transfer skills you already have, the more easily you can enter a new field without a period of transition or training. For instance, a number of career-changers I interviewed who had been managers or executives in the business world were able to move from their business jobs to management or executive jobs in the nonprofit sector. In those cases, they were able to transfer enough management, operational, or financial skills to make that transition directly (although the compensation in the nonprofit jobs often was lower).

Another option is to make a career change step-by-step. Elaine Cummings, who in her first career had taught business classes such as typing in a public high school, changed careers gradually. When Cummings returned to the paid workforce after some years as a stay-at-home mother, she used her secretarial skills (transferred from her earlier career teaching them) to explore several industries by working in them as a secretary. After Cummings found a work environment she liked—in the editorial offices of a magazine—and decided she wanted to enter publishing, she was able to learn by observing her colleagues and asking questions. With the perspective she got from working in office administration at a magazine and, in particular, from asking questions of her colleagues, Cummings could identify a career goal she'd someday like to attain: a job known as managing editor. She then also started to identify a path toward achieving that goal and set about to attain the skills she needed to move along the career path she'd chosen for herself. That career path involved self-study, learning from colleagues, picking up new skills on the job, taking a course, and, in her volunteer activities outside of work, taking on projects that could help her build additional skills. Eventually, over a period of ten to twelve years, Cummings achieved her goal of becoming a managing editor at a national magazine—and later became an editor in yet another industry: consulting. Cummings thus was able to change careers successfully from teaching business classes at a high school to editing by using a combination of transferable skills (which she used to enter a new industry) and then on-the-job learning and self-study. By learning while she was already working in publishing, Cummings was able to identify opportunities and pathways that would have been hard to see from outside that industry.

As the stories in this book illustrate, there are nearly as many approaches to career transition as there are people who change careers. Taking some time up front to think through your financial needs and current financial flexibility can help you craft an approach that works for you. Think creatively—about your resources, your needs, and the tactics you might use to change careers.

- Which of the five career-change scenarios described at the start of this chapter come closest to your situation? If you are seeking to earn more after career change, how much more money do you (realistically) hope to make? And if you are willing to earn less to have more satisfying work, what is the lowest long-term salary you would be comfortable with? (For example, if you currently earn $50,000 but could be content with $45,000, list $45,000.)

- Are there benefits that you currently receive in your job (health insurance, disability insurance, paid vacation) that are important to you or your family and so would be important to you to replicate in your next career? Are there some benefits you might be able to get other ways—for example, such as getting health insurance through a spouse's job? What are the trade-offs associated with that?

- What other nonmonetary factors are high priorities for you in your work situation? These might include a flexible schedule, a good working environment, a short commute, meaningful work, or other lifestyle factors.

- It will be easier to figure out your financial options if you have a good understanding of where your money goes. But many people don't. Do you have a good grasp of how your household spends its money? If not, you're not alone, but there are many budgeting tools available, and chances are you can find one that works for you. (For example, both of the books mentioned in the Resources box on page 68 offer an approach to getting a handle on your spending.)

what's been missing
from your work?

One of the most powerful career metaphors used in the twentieth century was the *career ladder*. Start at a low rung of your profession and company as a young person, the theory went, and you could move up over time, just as if you were climbing the rungs of a ladder. It was a great metaphor for times dominated by large corporations, economic growth, and employment stability—such as the period after World War II.

However, times have changed. Although the concept of a career ladder still has relevance in some settings, it makes less and less sense as a way of thinking about many careers. Downsizing, flatter organizations, and rapid organizational, economic, and technological change have all taken rungs out of many ladders—and pulled career ladders out from under many people in the middle of their careers. Whatever a typical career looks like today, it very often isn't a ladder.[1]

People have tried to come up with new, more fitting ways to describe what careers are like these days. Cliff Hakim, author of the book *We Are All Self-Employed: The New Social Contract for Working in a Changed World*, put forth the concept of a "career lattice" as a replacement metaphor for the career ladder. Movement on a ladder is limited to going either up or down; in contrast, Hakim notes, a lattice allows movement in a number of directions, including sideways. That kind of conceptual framework for thinking about careers, he indicates, is more appropriate than a ladder for an age in which people move around between various projects.[2] Mary Catherine Bateson, in her book *Composing a Life*, suggests that women's lives and work, in particular, are frequently not like a quest for a goal or a ladder one climbs. Instead, she observes, modern women's lives are often more like improvisational art—like a meal made out of ingredients already in the house or a patchwork quilt composed from a number of different fabrics. Although Bateson is writing especially about women—and the way their work often incorporates both work outside the home and family commitments—she notes that, in our era of rapid change, both men and women face the challenge of lives marked by interruptions and change.[3] And indeed, people who change careers voluntarily or are downsized from jobs due to industry shifts are often, as Bateson's metaphor suggests, doing a form of career improvisation, creating something new out of various elements of their work lives.

Another very useful metaphor for career transitions comes from the authors Richard J. Leider and David A. Shapiro, who wrote a book on life change called *Repacking Your Bags: Lighten Your Load for the Rest of Your Life*. These authors use the metaphor of carrying luggage full of things as you go through life; they point out that you can unpack your bags by deciding what components of your life you want to keep and what parts you want to leave behind—and then repack again by rethinking your priorities.[4] The image of unpacking and repacking is a very helpful way to think about today's turbulent career progressions. With this metaphor, each new project or job is seen as a new stage of a journey, not a rung on a ladder.

For career-changers, though, I think another career metaphor is particularly useful. Have you ever picked fruit? Think for a moment of that experience. Now imagine your life as a fruit-bearing tree, perhaps an apple or peach or orange tree. Every new direction you explore— whether a new job, a new kind of education or training you obtain, or a new hobby you pursue in your spare time—is like a branch of your tree that experiences new growth.

On many of the branches—in school, in each job you do, and in volunteer activities and hobbies—you develop new skills. Those may be specific skills such as a new language or computer program, people skills such as supervising or managing people, or organizational skills such as working with diverse groups of people or planning projects. Every time you learn to do something new, you're adding a new skill or competency. And each new skill is like your tree bearing a new fruit.

Now imagine you are picking some fruit from a tree—not gathering the whole harvest but just picking some fruit for eating or cooking. You don't restrict yourself to picking from only one branch of the tree, do you? Instead, you probably gather the best fruit for today's purpose from various branches of the tree. Something similar happens in career change. I find the fruit tree metaphor so helpful because I observed that many successful career-changers were, in fact, starting new careers using the "fruits" of a variety of branches of their lives, rather than just the primary skills from their most recent jobs.[5] Whether they are applying transferable skills from previous work in a new venue (something we'll discuss more in chapter 10), using knowledge or values they gained in childhood or from their family background, using skills or contacts gained outside of work, or returning to skills they used earlier in their career, many career-changers draw on knowledge and competencies they already have when they make a career switch—even a seemingly dramatic switch.

> As you contemplate career change, it's important to consider not just what skills you've used in your work recently and developed there but also this question: *what important parts of you have been missing from your most recent work?*

Accordingly, as you contemplate career change, it's important to consider not just what skills you've used in your work recently and developed there but also this question: *what important parts of you have been missing from your most recent work?*

drawing on earlier career skills or education

One possibility for career change is to use skills you developed earlier in your work life or in your education but have not been using much recently at work. For instance, Judy Goldberger had majored in Spanish in college, but when she worked as a fundraising campaign manager for a small nonprofit, she didn't use her Spanish in her job. But when Goldberger began to explore changing careers to become a nurse who would work with new mothers and babies, she found she particularly enjoyed working with immigrant women, who were often Spanish-speaking. Today, she works in the postpartum unit of a large urban hospital, and she often gets chances to use her Spanish as part of her new career.

bringing volunteer activities and hobbies into your work

Career-changers may also incorporate the "fruit" from other branches of their lives by incorporating into their paid work an activity that was previously a hobby or volunteer activity. For example, Lou Kobbs worked for many years at Digital Equipment Corporation, a computer company that grew to be a *Fortune* 500 company but then downsized as computer markets changed—and was acquired in 1998. While still working as a regional manager of training and operations at the company that acquired Digital, Kobbs became involved in a volunteer project in his free time, helping a friend and longtime colleague. Kobbs's friend and colleague, Fran Delaney, had been diagnosed with ALS (also known as Lou Gehrig's disease), a fatal neurological disease. After finding out he had ALS, Delaney started a fundraising effort with friends and family and set a goal of raising $1 million for ALS research. Kobbs was one of the friends who helped Delaney in a successful effort to do just that.[6]

Kobbs's role included working on launching a successful annual fundraising golf tournament. Ultimately, that volunteer work led Kobbs to an unexpected new career. Today Kobbs works in fundraising for the ALS Therapy Development Institute (www.als.net), a nonprofit working on treatments for ALS—and a big part of his job involves fundraising events.

Ellin Hanlon found a way to turn a hobby into a new career after she left her longtime employer during a corporate downsizing. Hanlon had worked primarily in office administration positions in the company, but one of her longtime loves was gardening, and she had built up considerable skills and knowledge in garden design. When her job was eliminated after the company where she worked was acquired, Hanlon took courses in landscape design and started her own landscape design business, Bright Ideas Garden Designs.

drawing on one aspect of prior work

In some cases, career-changers use skills from their most recent jobs in their new careers but draw more heavily on something that was just one aspect of that work. For example, at the large company where Carol Tienken worked for eighteen years, she worked primarily in marketing and sales forecasting. But in her last years at that company, Tienken worked on developing new international markets for the company's products—a job that involved a wide range of skills, including learning about supply chain management and doing inventories. That particular experience proved important when Tienken changed careers to become chief operating officer at the Greater Boston Food Bank, a large nonprofit food bank that distributes food to hunger relief agencies such as food pantries. The operations and warehouse skills that had been one part of Tienken's previous job played a larger role in her next job.

Similarly, Lee Finkle Estridge had a successful career as a sales rep who sold supplies such as photo albums to professional photographers. She saw understanding people's needs as key to being good at sales, and she became interested in psychology and personal development and started learning about it. Learning about personal development, in fact, became a "real passion" for her, she recalls. In the process, she came across the Enneagram, a tool for understanding personality types, and she found it helped her understand patterns of behavior. The interest in personal development that Finkle Estridge gained as part of her work as a sales rep—and her study of the Enneagram, which she became trained to teach about—were both things she used more extensively when she changed careers to become a personal coach.

drawing on family background

In addition to skills from previous work, schooling, hobbies, or volunteer work, there is another resource career-changers sometimes turn to: things they learned about work from their family background. For example, after Nick Pappas left his longtime employer in 1994, he needed to figure out what to do next; he had been working at the company, most recently as a manager in software services, since graduating from college in 1967. Pappas ultimately decided, after taking a few months off, to open an ice cream business. Although he had worked in the high-tech world for decades, his father had owned a diner, and Pappas had grown up around the food business and was familiar with it; he had worked in the diner as a youth. What's more, he had a cousin who owned an ice cream business in another state, and Pappas was able to work out a consulting arrangement with his cousin. Pappas paid his cousin; in return, the cousin agreed to share his recipes with Nick Pappas and teach him about making ice cream. Pappas thinks his cousin's help was important, because it allowed Pappas to start his business with a lot of knowledge about making high-quality ice cream.

Values you were taught as a child may also influence your choices when you make a career change. Jim Baroody changed careers from working as a manager in information technology and Internet-related industries to becoming a high-school math and computer teacher—and one factor for him was that his father had been a high-school teacher and guidance counselor in the town Baroody grew up in. Baroody had heard from former students about how much his father had meant in their lives, and his father's example had taught him that teaching could be an honorable profession. And when Gail Snowden left a longtime career as a banking executive after the bank where she had worked throughout her adult life was acquired, the values she was brought up with affected her decision to go into the nonprofit sector. Snowden's parents had started a nonprofit serving the inner city, and Snowden recalls that she was taught, as a child, that one person can make a difference in society—and that you have a responsibility to give back to society. In her career change, Snowden ended up working for several years for a charitable foundation that funded her city's nonprofits—work very much in line with the work her parents had done and with the values they had taught her. Now, she is the CEO of Freedom House, the nonprofit her parents founded.

resource

People sometimes feel that something is missing from their work life because they are in a line of work or kind of workplace that just doesn't suit their temperament. If you feel that's the case for you, a resource that can help you better understand how to find careers and workplaces that work well for your type of personality is the book *Do What You Are: Discover the Perfect Career for You Through the Secrets of Personality Type* by Paul D. Tieger and Barbara Barron (New York: Little, Brown, 4th ed., 2007). The authors use the conceptual framework of the Myers-Briggs, a well-known personality test, to help readers think about the kind of work that will suit their temperaments. The book is probably most useful in helping you think about the general type of work role you may thrive in and your career-related strengths and weaknesses; although the authors list possible careers for each personality type, they acknowledge that their lists of occupations are not comprehensive. The insights that *Do What You Are* offers into the workplace strengths and weaknesses of each personality type—and the components of work satisfaction for each type—can be extremely helpful. You can get a sample of the book's approach at the authors' website, **www.personalitytype.com**.

Of course, for many people changing careers, family background doesn't play a big role. If your parents weren't happy with their work—or you weren't happy with its effect on your family—it would stand to reason you might be less likely to emulate your parents' choices, for example. But in a culture in which career choices can be confusing—and the number of possibilities at times overwhelming—lessons you learned about the world of work from your family, or contacts or information you get from them now, can represent one more potential resource for you in a career change.

As the variety of stories in this chapter suggests, the ways people draw on their previous experiences and goals to build a satisfying career can be surprising—and the results unique to each person. Just as if you were approaching a tree full of beautiful ripe fruit, you have plenty of options to explore—and many resources to draw on.

for further reflection

Take some time to think about the "fruits" from various parts of your life—the skills and knowledge you've acquired not only from all the different jobs you've had but also from a combination of work, education, family, hobbies, and volunteering. One good way to do this is to use a set of large index cards, four inches by six inches. Or, if you prefer, you can either set aside some pages in your career change journal or use a spreadsheet for this exercise. At the top of each index card (or on top of a page in your career change journal or a column in your spreadsheet), list a job you have held that was *significant* for you. (That means you can skip the paper route you had in high school, unless it had some significant impact on you!) Then create an additional card labeled "Childhood," one labeled "High School," and one more card for each degree or course of study beyond high school that you undertook. Then create cards for experiences that have been important in your personal life, such as parenting, involvement in your religious community, travel, volunteer work, or hobbies. The important thing is that each card should represent a significant experience in your life, so add any other cards that come to mind.

Each index card represents a "branch" of your life. Now list some of the fruits you have received from each branch. Under each card title, list important things you learned from the experience; these could be a type of knowledge ("fluent Spanish" or "knowledge of the transportation industry"), certain skills or contacts, or personal traits and values. For example, if you had a job with an awful boss in which you learned great diplomacy, put your diplomacy skills on that job's branch. If you learned carpentry skills in high school, enjoy using them in your spare time, and always wished you could use those skills more, list your carpentry skills as fruits of a high school branch. If your parents taught you a strong work ethic that has served you well, list that on your childhood branch. Take your time doing this exercise.

Now look at the branches and fruits of your life and consider the following:

- What important parts of you—be they skills, values, or knowledge—have not been part of your paid work recently? Can you think of any that you would really like to try to incorporate into the work you do for a living?

- Are there things you have studied that you have not been using much in your work life but might like to incorporate more?

- Are there ambitions and career goals you once had that still have meaning for you? Are there variations on those goals that you might still be interested in pursuing?

- Are there skills, interests, information, values, or contacts from your family or upbringing that you could use in your career change?

- What kinds of knowledge, skills, abilities, or contacts do you have that are unusual? In what kind of work might they be advantageous?

PART II

CHARTING A NEW COURSE

In this next portion of the book, you'll explore the intersection between what you want and what the marketplace offers. You'll discover ways to find work you like that meets the practical requirements of your life and how to take advantage of economic trends. You'll consider ways to transfer skills from one kind of work to another. And, above all, you'll find out how to gain information about career options that interest you, through research and conversations with people already working in those careers. You'll also develop a framework for thinking about your career explorations as experiments—and identify low-risk ways you can learn about what particular careers are actually like.

The goal? *To discover techniques and strategies that will help you research and evaluate potential new careers.*

CHAPTER 8

meet your bliss halfway

Maybe you're lucky. Maybe you have a good idea of several new career possibilities you'd like to explore, and they are all ones for which workers are in high demand. With some training or experience, and some transferable skills you bring from your current work, you have good reason to believe that, in your new career, you can earn as much as or more than you do now. Or maybe you're changing careers at a time in your life when you don't need to earn as much as you do now.

But maybe that's not the case. What if you have a dream you are aching to pursue—something you think you might really love to do—but it doesn't seem very practical? Or perhaps you are not sure *what* you want to do next and are exploring a wide variety of options. How, in such cases, do you strike a balance between your ideal work and your financial needs and goals?

One oft-quoted piece of career advice is "follow your bliss," a phrase attributed to the late Joseph Campbell, who was a scholar of mythology.[1] There is a certain school of career (and career-change) thinking that has seeped into much of our popular consciousness; basically, it suggests that doing what you most love to do tends to lead to economic success. However, Campbell himself—who spent five years without a job during the Great Depression—apparently had a more complex view about the relationship between following one's bliss and economic success. When he taught at a school for boys and a student of his would ask if he could be a writer, Campbell said he would reply by saying, "I don't know. Can you endure ten years of disappointment with nobody responding to you, or are you thinking that you are going to write a best seller the first crack? If you have the guts to stay with the thing you really want, no matter what happens, well, go ahead."[2]

bliss and economics

That's quite realistic advice. The trouble with a career view that advocates following your passion and doing what you love to do is that it may not take enough account of the laws of supply and demand. Think about it: if everyone did the kind of work they most wanted to, without regard to compensation or demand for what the profession provides, the world would probably be full of artists and writers and actors and musicians and, sure, many gardeners, farmers, doctors, engineers, firefighters, chefs, and teachers, too. But there would, no doubt, be a noticeable shortage of garbage collectors, meter maids, prison guards, and people to work the late shift in factories and stores. Even middle managers might be in short supply. In such a world, you could probably buy beautiful, handmade jewelry on every street corner—but just try finding someone to clean up a hazardous waste spill, order office supplies, or drive a city bus at rush hour.

> The trouble with a career view that advocates following your passions and doing what you love to do is that it may not take enough account of the laws of supply and demand.

That's where the magic of supply and demand comes in. It can be hard to make a living as, say, an actor or musician—because so many people want to do that kind of work. As economist Steven D. Levitt and journalist Stephen J. Dubner point out in *Freakonomics: A Rogue Economist*

Explores the Hidden Side of Everything, glamorous, highly competitive professions like music and film function a lot like tournaments—with many people, often young, entering at the bottom and working hard at low wages in an attempt to win the prize of big success. More generally, Levitt and Dubner note, there are four significant elements that tend to determine how much a job pays: the number of "people willing and able to do a job . . . the specialized skills a job requires, the unpleasantness of a job, and the demand for services that the job fulfills."[3] If you think about it, those four elements are all about either the supply of people available to do a given job or the demand for such workers. As a result, it's generally much easier to make a living as, say, an accountant in the corporate world than as an actor or actress, because an accounting job requires significant skills and education and is often reasonably in demand—but may not have as much emotional and creative appeal to as great a number of people as working in the arts.

So although it would be nice to believe that doing what you love will lead to economic prosperity, that may not be the case. In interviewing career-changers, I didn't see any particularly strong correlation between how passionate someone was about enjoying the intrinsic nature of his or her new work and how much the person earned; those two factors didn't seem to be linked in any predictable way. Instead, the strongest typical correlation with compensation appeared to be occupation and field; not surprisingly, people who changed careers into occupations that pay well or for which there is good demand (or both) tended, on average, to make more money than people who changed into careers where it is often harder to make a good living.

It probably *is* true that, when doing work you really like to do, you may be more willing to put up with whatever difficulties or trade-offs the work requires. The trick, then, in career change—particularly if you have significant financial obliga-

> The trick in career change—particularly if you have significant financial obligations, such as children or a mortgage—is not so much to "follow your bliss" naively but rather to meet your bliss halfway and still pay the bills.

tions, such as children or a mortgage—is not so much to "follow your bliss" naively but rather to meet your bliss halfway and still pay the bills. The book title *Do What You Love, the Money Will Follow* is a classic and memorable phrase;[4] however, midlife career-changers may be wise to keep a slightly different motto in mind: "Do something you like that people will pay you for."

your career as a business

Think about it this way. In these economically uncertain times, your career is in many ways like a small business you run.[5] If you're looking for a new job, you're looking for a customer (in this case, an employer) who will buy your services for some period of time. If you're thinking of starting a business, you're obviously looking for customers. And even if you're starting or working for a nonprofit, you'll be looking for, in effect, "customers" willing to back the nonprofit with donations or grants. So as you think about career change, think of yourself as looking for an intersection between what you want to do and what people will pay you adequately for.[6]

Thinking in those terms certainly doesn't mean that you have to spend the rest of your working life in a career you dislike or that you have to give up your dreams of more satisfying work. You just need to make sure that your career plans have some kind of overlap with earning money (and, if further education is necessary, spending money to pay for education) that is comfortable for you.

If, for example, you are thinking of changing from a reasonably well-paying job to more fulfilling work in a field in which it's much harder to make a living, you should be prepared to earn less—and should think about whether you are willing to make trade-offs, such as adjusting your spending or having a greater reliance on a spouse's income. Alternatively, for some people,

> For some people, seemingly "nonblissful," mundane jobs can represent a very good career change choice, because they offer satisfying work with a better wage, good benefits, or a good advancement opportunity.

seemingly "nonblissful," mundane jobs can represent a very good career change choice, because they offer satisfying work with a better wage, good benefits, or a good advancement opportunity.

finding a balance

What does it look like when you find a good intersection between what you like to do and what people will pay you adequately for? Although every individual will answer that question differently, here are six possible approaches to seeking a good balance between dreams and financial obligations.

devote your existing skills to a cause you care about

Patrick Marshall is an example of someone who has been able to do this. In his twenties, Marshall worked in sales and business development in the computer networking and telecommunications industries, but then he made his first career change, into recruiting for the telecommunications industry. That recruiting job used his sales skills and gave him the opportunity to earn a good living, Marshall recalled. But then a confluence of events led to a very difficult period in Marshall's life. He and his wife discovered in 2000 that their baby daughter had cystic fibrosis. Then, in 2001, the telecom industry entered a downturn—and companies that aren't hiring don't, in turn, hire recruiting firms.

During this difficult period, Marshall began, as a concerned parent, to educate himself about cystic fibrosis. In the process, he discovered that there were a number of biotechnology companies doing research into developing cystic fibrosis treatments. What's more, Marshall realized as he researched the companies that a number of those biotech companies were in his region and—even in what was otherwise an economic downturn—had job openings listed on their websites.

Because of his daughter's illness, Marshall developed a newfound interest in biotechnology, which he sees as an industry that could lead to treatments that could help his daughter. After doing considerable research, Marshall concluded that there was an opportunity to launch a business doing recruiting for the growing biotech industry in his region. In 2001, he and a business partner launched a recruiting firm with that aim. Although biotechnology is hard for nonscientists to break into, Marshall had developed an intimate understanding of cystic fibrosis—and the company's first client was a company working on a treatment for cystic fibrosis.

Seven years later, Marshall reported that the business, StratAcuity Scientific, has grown to nine employees, plus fifteen or more contractors, and is flourishing. Although the company has expanded far beyond its initial cystic fibrosis niche, the fact that some of his client companies do research in cystic fibrosis (CF) is especially motivating for Marshall. "When we get the chance to work on a CF job, it's just thrilling," he said. In general, helping companies find scientists to do drug discovery work is very satisfying for Marshall, but it's especially so when the research involves cystic fibrosis. "I know that I'm doing the best I can with my abilities, professionally, for my daughter," he said. "That's the coolest thing."

By applying his existing skills as a recruiter to an industry that he especially cares about, Marshall has found a way to integrate skills with which he can earn a good living with something for which he has a real passion. That's a great combination. So ask yourself: is there a way I could use my existing skills in the service of something I particularly care about?

follow a passion that coincides with a promising career path

Even as a girl, Holly Gandolfo recalled, she had a passion for medicine. But as a young woman making career choices, Gandolfo also found herself frightened by the medical field; she thought it might be upsetting. So instead she majored in accounting and business in college. She married her high-school sweetheart, worked in reservations and customer service for a major airline, and had two children. But she still had an interest in medicine—and in her thirties she decided to go back to school, to a community college near her home, to become a nurse. Today Gandolfo works in a hospital as an RN, a job she is very happy with.

For Gandolfo, following her career dream was also a good career move, because the particular occupation that she wanted to enter—nursing—is one for which demand is very high. In part because of an aging population, the number of jobs for registered nurses in the United States is projected to grow about 29 percent between 2004 and 2014.[7] As a career-changer, if you have a dream that coincides with a growing market in which employees are in high demand, you may be well positioned to follow that dream. (We'll discuss growing markets in more detail in chapter 9.)

find a practical variation of something you love to do

When she was growing up, playing music was a big part of Robin Flint's life. But she gave it up in college. "I literally didn't play the piano for twenty years," she said. Then her fortieth birthday came around. Flint, who at the time was working as a medical secretary but thinking of changing careers, decided to buy a piano for that birthday. Buying the piano "just woke everything up. I remembered everything I loved about playing piano and having music in my life," she recalled. Flint got into a conversation with the piano technician who came to tune the piano—and, watching her at work, Flint realized that piano tuning looked like a kind of work she might do, since she wanted to work with tools and with her hands. Ultimately, Flint decided to go back to school to become a piano tuner—a trade she practices today. Working as a piano technician has allowed Flint to do work related to pianos and music. "I love pianos," she explained. "I have no illusions of being a [professional] musician or anything: I don't play that well. But taking care of them and fixing them is such a great way to express my love for the instrument."

Thinking about practical variations of what you love to do can be particularly helpful when you are starting a career change. Don McKillop, for example, used to be a vice president at a bank and now is an artist. He undertook that career change after he left the bank where he had worked for many years when there was a reorganization at the company. For a while after leaving the bank, McKillop was unsure of his next step. He had always enjoyed drawing and painting, and he thought about how he could earn money from art. McKillop, who has an MBA, began by combining his art and business skills to develop an art-related small business. His niche? It occurred to McKillop that real estate brokers might buy an artist's portrait of a client's new home, to give as a gift to the home buyer. So for five years he ran a busy home-portrait business. Eventually, with the support of his wife, Susan Davy, who also has an MBA, McKillop stopped doing the home-portrait work to have time to do other kinds of art and develop a body of work to exhibit. He now sells his art in galleries. McKillop thinks that the home-portrait business helped make his transition into the art world easier. In starting an art-related small business initially, he was able to leverage his business savvy to develop a transitional career solution that incorporated

resources

The Internet is a wonderful tool for starting to compare different potential careers. One particularly helpful tool is a career website sponsored by the U.S. Department of Labor, **www.careeronestop .org**. At that website, click on the section for "Browse Occupation" and try the "Occupation Profile" tool. With it, you can select an occupation and the state you live in (or plan to live in) and get information such as a description of what people in that occupation do, what skills they need, how much they typically make (nationally and, often, in your state), and how much employment in that occupation is projected to grow or decline in the next few years (both nationally and, often, in your state). An additional handy factor: the occupational profiles often have links to profiles of other, related occupations, so you can start to compare and learn about related occupations in a field. The "Occupation Profile" tool will be less useful to you if you have a very specialized career goal in mind or one that can't be easily categorized, but it's quite helpful if you're exploring common careers.

Another resource, **www.jobstar.org**, includes numerous salary surveys.

important elements of his career goal—in that he was working professionally as an artist.

If finding a practical variation on something you love to do sounds like an appealing approach to you, ask yourself: What are some occupations related to my dream? What are some ways people make money in the field?

combine two careers

Yet another possibility is to combine two careers, so that you can balance a desire to do work you love with your need to earn money. You'll find more details about the two-career option, and people who have chosen it, later in the book in chapter 14.

identify a general goal, then find the best specific opportunity

A couple of successful career-changers I spoke with said they first identified a general work goal that they'd like—such as doing work in a helping profession or owning a small business—and then evaluated several interesting jobs or opportunities that met their general criterion. That approach allows you to try to create an optimal combination of several variables—not only intrinsic enjoyment of the work, but also other factors such as economic compensation and chances for success—rather than simply maximizing the extent to which you enjoy the work itself.

be open to new possibilities

When Greg McCormick got a college degree in biology, he initially thought he'd train further and become a physical therapist; he even did an internship in that field. But at the time he graduated from college in 1998, he thought the starting salaries being offered for physical therapists were too low to make going to graduate school for the career a good choice for him (although, he says, salaries for physical therapists subsequently improved). He wasn't sure what to do next, so he worked in construction, the industry his father worked in.

Then McCormick started hearing that the physician assistant profession was promising. (A physician assistant is a professional who provides medical care under a doctor's supervision.) When McCormick began to seek out more information about becoming a physician assistant, both a physical therapist he knew and his former college adviser were encouraging; both told him the physician assistant profession could be a good option for him. McCormick did decide to become a physician assistant, which is currently projected to be one of the fastest-growing occupations in America in coming years.[8] Almost six years after finishing graduate school, McCormick loves his work as a physician assistant in a surgical practice. "I think it's the most amazing job," he said.

> By evaluating job market circumstances, you may, through your career explorations, identify a promising career path that you hadn't initially considered.

By evaluating job market circumstances—and by asking people knowledgeable about healthcare for insights about professions in the industry—McCormick was able to find an option that was better for him than his original career plan. Like McCormick, you may, through your career explorations, identify a promising career path that you hadn't initially considered.

The bottom line? Following your bliss may *sound* appealing, at least at first. But for many career-changers, it's important to think about not only what you most like to do but also where your skills, interests, aptitudes, and dreams fit into today's economy. With some creative thinking, you can hopefully find ways to both do work you enjoy and meet your household's financial needs.

- What are some career dreams you have or have had in the past (including in your childhood and young adulthood)? What, in a few words, did you find appealing about those potential careers?

- Can you think of ways in which you may be able to find a satisfying intersection between what you'd like to do now and what people will pay you for?

- If you are interested in some careers for which you know little about the compensation in the field or the demand for workers, here's a very preliminary step to learning more. (We'll talk about more in-depth steps in later chapters.) Use the "Occupation Profile" tool at the **www.careeronestop.org** website to learn more about some careers that appeal to you (see the Resources box on page 95). Take notes in your career change journal on what you find out about the occupations that interest you. Feel free to read about any related jobs that sound interesting to you and take notes on those, too.

identifying growing markets

Have you ever gone swimming in a body of water—such as a river or ocean—in which there's a current? Swim in one direction, and it's surprisingly effortless: you make progress so quickly it's surprising. But when you turn around to swim back, a funny thing happens: it's much, much harder on the way back, and it's not just because you're tired. It's because of the current. Swim with the current, and everything is easier. But try to swim against the current, and it takes much more effort to make headway.

Job markets—much like oceans and rivers—have currents. Job markets are affected by economic trends, both large and small. And looking for a job or starting a business in a market that's undergoing substantial growth is like swimming with the current pushing you along. Looking for a job or starting a business in a field that's very competitive or is contracting, on the other hand, is like swimming against the current. You can do it—but it won't be nearly as easy

> Looking for a job or starting a business in a market that's undergoing substantial growth is like swimming with the current pushing you along. Looking for a job or starting a business in a field that's very competitive or is contracting, on the other hand, is like swimming against the current.

to make progress as it would if you were in a growing job market, with the current pushing you along.

In many job hunts, people with experience in a field may be able to transcend competitive conditions in that field; after all, their years of experience and contacts can give them an advantage. But when you're changing careers, you may have an easier time if you can find a way to get into an occupation—or an industry, an industry niche, or an organization—that's growing. The reason? If more people are needed this year in a particular field than were needed last year, there's usually more room for new people to join than if the field is stagnant or shrinking. Even if you are entering an occupation or industry that isn't growing much, there may be submarkets—market niches—or organizations where employment is growing more rapidly.

I first realized the extreme importance of growing markets to economic opportunity while working for a number of years as a writer and editor at *Inc.* magazine. *Inc.* is one of the leading U.S. small-business management magazines, and each year it publishes a list of the fastest-growing privately held companies in the United States. (For many years, this list was called the *Inc.* 500, but it's since been expanded and is currently called the *Inc.* 5,000.) On several occasions, I wrote articles about the *Inc.* 500 list and, in particular, the economic trends reflected in it.

As I studied the *Inc.* 500 list, I realized that the list—which was essentially a list of entrepreneurial companies, often young, that had been growing very, very fast in recent years—showcased "hot spots" in the economy. Although there would typically be some companies in "ordinary" markets on the *Inc.* 500 list, they weren't the majority; not surprisingly, *Inc.* 500 companies were disproportionately in fast-growing markets. And being in fast-growing markets made it easier for the small companies that made the *Inc.* 500 list to grow fast, too.[1]

Now, when you think about your career, you don't necessarily need or want to seek out the fastest-growing markets; your aim, after all, is to find work that satisfies you, not just work that's in the highest demand. Besides, as Richard Nelson Bolles, author of the career guide *What Color Is Your Parachute?* has pointed out, there are problems with forecasts

resource

Does the concept of thinking about markets, trends, and opportunities seem alien to you? Check out the *Inc.* 5,000 list of fast-growing privately held companies at **www.inc.com/inc5000** to get a sense of how trends can create economic opportunity. You can search the list by industry or state, then click on each company name to read a capsule profile that explains why that company grew. The lessons may not be directly translatable to growth in the future—after all, the list covers growth in the recent past—but its helpful practice in thinking about trends and the way they shape economic opportunities.

about occupational demand, in part because job markets are always in flux between a shortage and a surplus of workers. This makes it difficult to forecast both the future demand for workers in any given occupation and the future supply of such workers.[2]

But with that caveat, there are nonetheless two questions about market dynamics that are helpful to keep in mind as you explore career change. First: *is the market I'm thinking of entering growing and likely to grow over the long term?* If the answer is no, that by itself doesn't mean you shouldn't enter a field; it's simply that if the answer is yes, your career change may be easier. All other things being equal, it's just plain easier to change careers if you enter a field that's growing. Second: *is the market I'm currently in—and thinking of leaving—shrinking or likely to shrink over the long term?* People are sometimes prompted to change careers because the occupation or industry—or even just the organization—in which they have been working has begun to shrink or decline, whether temporarily or permanently. Being in an industry, organization, or occupation that is declining in size can be like taking part in an unpleasant game of musical chairs, in which a job equals a chair. In a declining job market, every year there are fewer and fewer chairs, so not everybody gets to find or keep one. Even a market that is going through a downturn—but that will later rebound—may prompt workers in it to change careers; such workers, in effect, opt not to wait out the downturn.

Patrick Marshall, whose story of starting a recruiting firm specializing in biotechnology was featured in chapter 8, is an example of someone who changed careers into a growth market from one that was in a recession at the time. When his work doing recruiting for the telecommunications industry was suffering because of an industry downturn in 2001, Marshall noticed that biotech companies were growing and hiring at that time. What's more, Marshall had learned that, as a recruiter, he could get a sense of future growth and hiring trends at high-tech start-up companies by tracking the investments being made by venture capitalists—professional investors who fund high-technology start-ups. Because of his research on venture capital investment trends, Marshall could see that, over time, venture capitalists were increasing their investments in biotechnology start-up companies. In switching from telecom recruiting to biotech recruiting, then, Marshall was changing from an industry going through a recession to one that was growing at that point. And he sees a need for the company he cofounded, StratAcuity Scientfic, to continue to change with the market, entering new fields such as the convergence of biotech and nanotechnology. "It's an evolving thing," Marshall explained. "That's why, when we started StratAcuity, we didn't name it anything overly specific."

Like Marshall, Carol Tienken changed careers to a work situation that offered better growth prospects than her former job did at the time. In Tienken's case, the company where she had worked for many years began to experience dramatic changes—and decline—in its primary market as a result of new technologies that changed that market. Tienken, who had started work in marketing at the company in her early twenties, was fortunate. When her project developing new markets in Latin America for the company was cancelled in 1998, Tienken said, her boss offered her a choice of being reassigned to another project within the organization or taking a severance package. She took the severance package and left the company in late 1998, after working there for eighteen years. Several years later, Tienken's former employer filed for Chapter 11 bankruptcy. (The company was subsequently acquired and developed a new strategy.)

After leaving her longtime employer, Tienken wasn't sure exactly what she wanted to do next, so she conducted informational interviews with people in a variety of fields. (Informational interviews are meetings in which you ask people working in a field that interests you to talk with you about their work, so you can learn more about it.)[3] One field that interested Tienken was the nonprofit sector, so she explored it as part of her informational interviewing. In late 1998 Tienken conducted an informational interview at the Greater Boston Food Bank, a regional nonprofit food bank that distributes food to food pantries. It turned out the food bank was growing and needed to hire a chief operating officer. Tienken applied and ultimately was offered the position in April 1999. She has continued to be COO of the Greater Boston Food Bank, and the organization where she works has continued to grow.

Growing organizations often offer good opportunities; so can occupations in growing markets. For example, as mentioned in chapter 8, when Holly Gandolfo changed careers into nursing, she was choosing a field that generally offers good job opportunities at this time—in part because of an aging population. Of course, you shouldn't choose a career or industry just because it's growing; after all, there's no sense changing careers to work in a field you dislike. And many people decide to stay in professions they like even if opportunities are becoming harder to come by, whether because of a temporary economic downturn like a recession or because of a longer-term structural decline. It's also worth noting that trends are hard to predict, and today's boom industry may have a downturn later, for reasons that cannot now be foreseen. In particular, industries can go through a rapid growth period followed by a temporary shakeout—like the shakeout that happened with Internet-related business in the early 2000s. The Internet "bubble" burst then, but Internet-related markets such as online advertising and e-commerce subsequently continued, over time, to exhibit longer-term growth.

However, even given the difficulty of predicting long-term trends, it's definitely worth considering whether any of the fields you'd like to enter is in a growing market—or whether there is a growing submarket within it. You also should try to distinguish between short-term fads and fashions and long-term trends. Fads and short-term fashions may come and go, but longer-term trends are worth paying attention to.

What does a long-term trend look like? While there are many long-term economic trends, here are just a few examples of trends that economists at the U.S. Bureau of Labor Statistics think will affect job markets in the United States in the years between 2006 and 2016:

- As the baby boom generation ages, the portion of the U.S. population aged fifty-five and over is expected to increase by twenty million, reaching eighty-seven million by 2016 (an increase of about 30 percent). As a group, people aged fifty-five and older use more healthcare and social services than other age groups—as a result, jobs in healthcare and social assistance sectors are expected to be fast growing over the coming decade. The aging of the population has other implications as well, such as a need for more personal financial advisors to help people manage their retirement savings.

- Our society continues to rely increasingly on complex computer systems. As a result, the Bureau of Labor Statistics is projecting that computer and mathematics-related jobs will increase rapidly, by about 25 percent, during the decade—despite the fact that more routine computer programming jobs are increasingly being moved offshore.

- A combination of concern about the environment and environmental regulations is projected to lead to growing demand for environmental engineers, scientists, and technicians. In particular, the job category known as "environmental science and protection technician" (including those in healthcare) is expected to be one of the thirty fastest-growing occupations between 2006 and 2016.[4]

One good way to think about trends is to recognize that virtually any type of change creates opportunity for someone—the question is, for whom. For example, even something as awful as global warming and climate change will probably create career opportunities. Scientists are predicting that climate change will lead to more frequent extreme weather events such as powerful hurricanes, intense precipitation, and severe droughts.[5] In the long term, that may mean more work for disaster relief providers, for engineers working on combating problems caused by climate change, and for alternative energy companies in industries such as wind and solar power.

So, more generally, a good question to ask as you look at an occupation or industry is, *What changes are affecting that industry or occupation and where do they create opportunities?* This question may help you identify growing niches or opportunities.

the bottom line

As you research occupations and industries that interest you and talk to people in them, you'll want to keep questions like these in mind:

- Is this industry or occupation growing as a whole?
- If not, are there segments or organizations that are growing?
- What kinds of long-term trends are affecting this industry, organization, or occupation?

Armed with this kind of information, you don't need to try to swim against the current in your new career. Instead, you can choose to let economic trends help carry you to success.

resource

You can find a list of the fastest-growing occupations in the United States, and other employment trends, in the "Browse Occupations" section of the U.S. Department of Labor–sponsored CareerOne Stop site, **www.careeronestop.org**. See www.careeronestop.org/ExploreCareers/Occupations/OccupationsWhatsHot.aspx.

1. The more you think about how trends affect job markets, the better you'll get at spotting opportunities. A good way to practice thinking about economic trends and growing markets is to start by thinking about the industry in which you have been working, as you know it well already. (You can then apply the same type of thinking to new careers as you explore them.) Would you characterize your current industry as an industry that is generally experiencing better growth than the economy as a whole; a mature, established industry that grows only as fast (or as little) as the economy does; or a declining industry that is actually shrinking over the long term? How has that affected you? How will that affect your future prospects?

2. Now think about the occupation (that is, the type of job you do) in which you have been working. Is demand for it generally growing a lot, growing a little, staying the same, or shrinking? (In some cases, the growth prospects for your occupation will be very similar to those of your industry. But in other cases— for example, if you're an accountant or human resources professional—you have the opportunity to work in a variety of industries.)

3. What are some trends affecting your current industry? Are there any growing niches in your industry? What are they?

4. What are some trends affecting your current occupation? Are there any growing niches that you are aware of?

5. How much do you know about the growth prospects of other career possibilities that interest you? What trends are affecting those occupations or industries? (If you don't know the answers to those questions yet, don't worry. Just keep them in mind as you further research each career possibility you're considering.)

use your skills, strengths, and constraints

Kathie Simmons faced a challenge in her job hunt. She had worked in the food industry for years. But shortly after the terrorist attacks on September 11, 2001, the U.S. economy went into a downturn—and as people started eating out less, Simmons explained, she was laid off from her job as a restaurant manager for a food-service company.

Simmons's challenge? She had not had the opportunity to learn a lot of computer skills while working at her longtime job, and she was concerned that she would not be able to find a comparable job without better computer skills. So Simmons visited a local One-Stop Career Center to get assistance with her job hunt. (There are One-Stop Career Centers, designed to help job-hunters, located throughout the United States. Although the centers' names vary, the One-Stop Career Centers program is coordinated by the U.S. Department of Labor's Employment and Training Administration. For information about how to find One-Stop Career Centers, see the Resources section toward the end of this chapter.)

At the One-Stop Career Center, Simmons found out that she could apply for a training voucher to pay for additional training; at the time, there was some special job-training funding available for people laid off in the aftermath of the September 11 terrorist attacks. With the training voucher, Simmons, who did not have a college degree, was able to qualify for an office skills training course offered by a local nonprofit; she took part in a program that, over the course of a number of months of full-time classes, helped her improve her computer skills and other office skills, such as keyboard typing.

As part of the training program, Simmons did an unpaid internship at an office at a university. She liked the internship and determined to try to work as hard as she could to get a job at the university; she was so determined to do so that she kept coming to work after the internship ended. Simmons's strategy was successful: she applied for a job opening at the university, and in the summer of 2002 she got a job as an administrative assistant in an academic department.

When she was laid off from her food-service job, Simmons recalled, "I didn't really know about this thing called 'transferable skills.'" But in the process of training for a new career, Simmons learned something important: she had lots of transferable skills. Working as a manager in one setting—food service—had taught her administrative skills that she could take with her to new work in a quite different setting. Her transferable skills ranged from customer service skills to managing billing and schedules.

What's more, once she was working in the university setting, Simmons was exposed to other career opportunities; after a while, she transferred to another administrative assistant position in another department. There, she's been able to not only use her existing office skills but also gain new ones; her current job duties include updating a website, for example. Simmons, who has since added additional job duties and become an executive assistant, remains very satisfied with her new career, which, she noted, has better benefits, a better salary, and a better schedule than her work in the food industry.

skills you can take with you

Simmons's story illustrates an important lesson for career-changers. Even if you change the type of work you do when you change careers—and even if you do have to learn some new skills—you can also bring skills from your previous work with you. You aren't starting from scratch, the way you did when you first entered the workforce as a young person. Even people who change careers to what seems like a completely different line of work often find that they have important skills that they can transfer.

The prevalence of transferable skills is very positive news for career-changers. Consider the story of Jim Pitts. In the mid-1990s, Pitts made a truly dramatic career change: from sales manager for a large technology company to organic farmer. It's hard to think of a much more radical career change than that! From working with people in a corporate environment, Pitts switched to working with his hands a great deal—working with vegetables and the earth. How could two such different lines of work involve transferable skills?

> Even people who change careers to what seems like a completely different line of work often find that they have important skills that they can transfer.

Even in that very substantial career change, Pitts found he used skills from his previous career. At first he thought about starting his farm with a business model called "community supported agriculture" that is popular with many small organic farms and that focuses on selling directly to local consumers, who sign up to buy a portion of the farm's produce each season. But Pitts knew a lot about corporate sales, so he instead began approaching supermarkets in his area about carrying his produce. Although some other small-scale organic farmers might not have had the knowledge about how to sell to supermarket managers—or the desire to do so—Pitts was right at home doing that; after all, as a former sales manager for a large corporation, he had years of experience selling to managers in large organizations. "I could do the 'corporate-speak,'" he said. Pitts was able to transfer corporate sales skills from his old career into this new arena, and he began successfully selling his organic vegetables to local supermarkets. Pitts also has found that he uses his people skills in selling at a local farmers' market and in running a bed-and-breakfast that is now part of the farm operations. "Skills that you have are *always* applicable to something else," he explained. "And it's leveraging that that is a key to success."

Lois Ford and Lou Ciercielli, a married couple introduced in chapter 4, are also people who transferred skills during a significant career change. Trained as mechanical engineers, they once both worked as managers at a *Fortune* 500 company, in a division making industrial turbines. They gradually changed careers and now run a baking company in rural New Hampshire, where they make products like brownies and cookies that are sold through venues like mail-order catalogs. Like Pitts's transition, theirs was a fairly substantial career change. But Ford and Ciercielli say they have been able to transfer their knowledge of manufacturing management from their previous line of work to their current career. "The factory system, the inventory systems—it's no different," Ford said.

Both of these stories involve substantial career changes—and yet the career-changers still found they had important transferable skills. Generally, the closer the change you are considering is to the kind of work you have done up until now, the more skills you likely will be able to transfer from your current field to the new one. And in addition to skills, you may possess what I call *intangible assets* from your previous work that may be transferable. I'm not talking here about assets like money or other forms of financial wealth (although those certainly help in making a career change!) but instead about, say, a network of people you know and who trust you, or knowledge of a particular market or group. Those are intangible assets that you may be able to bring to your new type of work.

many ways to transfer skills

There are all kinds of ways you can transfer skills or intangible assets when you make a change in your career. Which of the following might apply to you and the type of career change you're considering?

1. **You can do the same job, or a similar job, in a different industry or sector.** This is one of the most straightforward types of career change you can make. When you are changing industries but not the type of job you do, your transferable skills are usually clear; what remains is for you to convince others that you can easily handle the transition and get up to speed on the new industry. Patrick Marshall, whose story was described in chapters 8 and 9, made this type of industry change when he transitioned from being a recruiter for the telecommunications industry to launching a recruiting firm specializing in the biotechnology industry. To make the transition easier, Marshall and his business partner hired a consultant to help them adapt their recruiting style to biotechnology. Marshall also learned about the new industry by doing a lot of reading and by talking to people in the field, by phone and in person, and asking them questions. That, in fact, is a process he continues to this day.

2. **You can move to a different type of job in the same organization or industry.** This is a common type of career change and one that can happen fairly naturally, as you use your status as an insider within an organization or industry to learn about new opportunities.

3. **You can use the same or similar technical skills in a different context, with different applications and job duties.** This type of career change, too, is one in which you will likely be able to transfer significant skills—although the work may also require some additional skills and the ability to adapt to a new environment. For example, Lisa MacLean, who had worked

as a computer professional and had a master's degree in her field, changed careers to teach computer science at a college. Although teaching is a very different job from network administration and computer programming, MacLean is still using her information technology knowledge and skills.

4. **You can transfer personal or people skills—such as management, marketing, sales, or problem-solving skills—to a different job in a different environment.** Such skills are among the easiest to transfer—in fact, you may transfer these skills almost automatically to whatever line of work you go into. If you have happily used skills such as marketing, leadership, or negotiating long enough, they probably have become part of your personal repertoire—no matter what kind of work you do. And you can apply personal or people skills in very different contexts. For example, Art Mellor, an engineer who was educated at MIT (Massachusetts Institute of Technology) and who had cofounded several technology companies, transferred a number of leadership, entrepreneurial, and problem-solving skills when he decided to change careers. Mellor was diagnosed with multiple sclerosis (MS) when he was in his thirties; at the time, he was working as chief technology officer of a start-up company he had cofounded. He began to educate himself about the disease—and became concerned about how little researchers knew about what causes MS. As an engineer and an entrepreneur, Mellor was used to tackling problems through a logical method: by finding out what causes them and then developing a solution and a plan to implement it, with milestones and measurable steps. He also had experience starting and growing organizations as part of a team of founders.

After his diagnosis, Mellor thought about going back to school to get a biology degree so he could become an MS researcher himself. But he realized that he could instead bring his business skills and engineering practices to helping organize the MS research already being done. So, together with a medical cofounder, Mellor founded the Accelerated Cure Project for

Multiple Sclerosis, a nonprofit organization that looks at the big picture in MS research—and seeks to accelerate research into the causes of MS by organizing information about MS research and fostering collaboration among researchers.

5. **You can use your general aptitudes and talents in a different context.** Is there something you really have a knack for? For example, you may be good at working with your hands, at working with words, with numbers, with mechanical or engineering challenges, or with people. You may be naturally artistic or particularly good at organizing space. These are all examples of general talents that you may be able to use in a new career.

6. **You can also transfer skills or knowledge in a number of other ways.** For example, you can transfer knowledge of a particular industry or set of customers. You can use personal contacts acquired in a previous career. Or, as discussed in chapter 7, you can bring skills acquired in some other part of your life—such as hobbies, volunteer work, or education—into your work life for the first time.

use your strengths— and your limitations, too

As you think about how you might employ your skills and talents in your next career, a good question to keep in mind is: what are your strengths? Research has found that workplace teams in which employees get to use their strengths every day are more likely to be productive.[1] Marcus Buckingham, who has written extensively about the concept of personal strengths, suggests that you can identify your own strengths by looking for activities for which the following is true: you have success in the activity; you are drawn to it instinctively; you feel happy and focused doing it, and it's easy to concentrate; and finally, it fills an emotional need of yours and feels right.[2]

Still not sure what your strengths are? In his book *Let Your Life Speak*, Parker J. Palmer writes that we often need help from others to identify our own gifts and talents—because they are things that come so naturally to us that "we are no more conscious of having them than we are of breathing."[3]

Although it's important to think about your strengths when changing careers, it's also important to think about your constraints. If you're like many adults already in the workforce, odds are good that you have some constraints and limitations on the next career you choose. Those constraints may be money (for example, you may not have all the money you'd like for education or launching a business) or time (you may be tied down with family and work responsibilities that limit your flexibility to take on certain kinds of jobs or training), or they may involve geography (you and your family may be committed, at least for the near future, to a certain geographical area, which may limit the type of career you pursue next). In some cases, age can be a constraint (in that it may affect how you think about physically demanding careers or careers that require many additional years of training).

Sound depressing? Here's the good news. It's not. *Contrary to what you might think, constraints and limitations aren't necessarily a problem when you're changing careers.* In fact, your constraints may actually be helpful to you when changing careers—because they can help you choose or rule out particular courses of action or directions. What's the key to using your constraints constructively when changing careers? Don't kid yourself. Figure out what your constraints are—then figure out how to compensate for them or work around them.

> Your constraints may actually be helpful to you when changing careers—because they can help you choose or rule out particular courses of action or directions.

Admittedly, that idea runs contrary to some popular beliefs, at least in the United States. In the land of opportunity, we like to believe that people will succeed if they simply follow their dreams, bliss, or passion. But, as we've discussed in chapter 8, following your bliss blindly can be a problematic approach for career-changers. In contrast, looking your constraints straight in the eye and figuring out an approach that works around them is a technique that can lead to successful outcomes.

How does such an approach look in practice? Here are several examples of successful career-changers who worked within the boundaries of their constraints to build new careers:

- Nick Pappas, whose story was introduced in chapter 4, was interested in starting a small business after he stopped working at his longtime employer, which had gone through a number of rounds of downsizing. One of the businesses Pappas considered starting was an ice cream store—for which he could draw on the expertise of a cousin who had a similar business in another state. Pappas worked out a consulting arrangement with his cousin, paying him to learn the ropes and use his ice cream flavors. Pappas's reasoning? He was already fifty years old— and he thought it would take fifteen to twenty years to develop ice cream recipes like his cousin's. In hindsight, Pappas, who founded and runs an ice cream business called Lizzy's, thinks that his decision to enlist his cousin's help was key—and that he would have failed if he had not taken that step.

- Teresa Bell, a high school graduate who had been a homemaker and worked part-time outside the home while raising her children, decided to go back to school to prepare for a new career after she and her husband separated and began divorce proceedings. With two school-age children, Bell decided her best bet in training for a new career was the community college located near her, because it was both convenient to her home and relatively inexpensive. So she went to the library and studied the community college course catalog in conjunction with career reference books that describe various jobs. To identify a new career, Bell cross-referenced the programs of study in the community college course catalog with the job descriptions and salary and job demand information in career reference books like the *Occupational*

Outlook Handbook. In that way, she compared the various career path options she could prepare for at the local community college, and from those options successfully chose what became her next career. Bell chose to study radiologic technology and then earned an associate degree in that field at the community college. She has now been working happily as a radiologic technologist at a nearby hospital for almost eight years.

- Ethan Becker was laid off from his job as marketing director at a digital video company during an economic downturn. It was August; his wife was pregnant with twins and had already quit her job as a pre-kindergarten teacher so she could stay home with the children after they were born. (The twins were born in October.) To support his family, Becker needed to figure out his next career move. At that point Becker's father invited his son to join the family business—a small communications training company called the Speech Improvement Company, Inc. Seven years later, Becker is still working at the family business, as a senior speech coach and trainer—and enjoying it. In the meantime, while working, he completed an MBA through an online program, and he is now writing a book about mastering communication in the workplace. In retrospect, Becker thinks getting laid off from his marketing job was a blessing in disguise. "Sometimes we make our best decisions during the hardest of times," he observed.

- After Kathie Newhall had her third child, she no longer wanted to work at a full-time administrative job in the big city that was a long commute from her home. She wanted work that would allow her the flexibility to be available for her children after school. First she found a part-time job as a secretary to a magnet salesman. And that work later helped lead Newhall to her next career: running a small business, Holiday Hang-ups, Inc., which makes magnetic hooks that enable people to hang wreaths on steel or single-pane glass doors.

To test her business idea, Newhall started small; she approached garden center stores about selling the magnetic device and initially based the business out of her home. After a small initial investment, she financed the business's gradual growth out of its earnings—a constraint that she thinks forced her to grow more slowly in the early stages of her business and to do her homework. ("Sometimes, not having a lot

resources

A quick resource for learning more about transferable skills is the Quintessential Careers website. You can read articles about the topic at **www.quintcareers.com/transferable_skills.html**.

The classic career guide *What Color Is Your Parachute?* by Richard Nelson Bolles has some great exercises to help you identify your transferable skills. In the 2008 edition, you'll find the section on transferable skills in chapter 13, "The Three Secrets to Finding That Dream Job of Yours." Another resource: the *What Color Is Your Parachute Workbook*, also by Bolles, includes transferable-skills identification exercises, but in a handy workbook format.

Interested in finding out about what your local One-Stop Career Center has to offer? To find the One-Stop Career Center nearest you, use the search function at **www.careeronestop.org/findos**.

Want to see how other career-changers transfer skills from one field to another? Are you trying to figure out how to market your own transferable skills during a career change? Here are two good books about resumes for career-changers. Both can help you think about how to position your transferable skills on a resume, when looking for a new type of work: *Expert Resumes for Career Changers* by Wendy S. Enelow and Louise M. Kursmark (Indianapolis: JIST Works, 2005) and *The Career Change Resume* by Kim Isaacs and Karen Hofferber (New York: McGraw-Hill, 2003).

Both of these useful books contain lots of sample resumes organized by general job goal. Both books also share some advice in common, such as the observation that it's often helpful for career-changers to use a resume format that includes not only a chronological employment history but also a summary of relevant skills and qualifications. As an added benefit, there's a chapter in *Expert Resumes for Career Changers* on how to present resumes in various formats: in e-mail, as a printed document, as a scannable document, or on the Web.

of financial resources can kind of be a blessing," she observed.) Newhall has now been running her business successfully for more than fifteen years. Over the years she has sold her products in a range of venues, including through QVC, the television shopping company.

In all four of these cases, successful career-changers looked thoughtfully at a constraint in their lives—such as age or family responsibilities—and developed approaches that worked within the constraints they faced—and, as a result, worked for them. Although it is certainly possible to have so many constraints in your life that it is hard to develop good new career options, having a few limitations is not necessarily a problem. In fact, some researchers believe that facing resource constraints can encourage innovative thinking.[4] So use your skills, use your strengths—and use your constraints, too! By taking them all into account, you can develop a new career path that works for you and your situation.

for further reflection

- What do you see as some of your strengths and talents? Try asking friends, loved ones, and people you've worked with what they see as your particular gifts and talents; you may, as Parker Palmer suggests, find that others will identify gifts that come so naturally to you that you aren't very aware of them.

- Review the index cards you developed in chapter 7—the ones that list skills, knowledge, and insights you've gained through various aspects of your life. Now list several occupations that you think might interest you. Can you think of any ways you might apply some of your skills, talents, or knowledge to those careers?

- What are some of the constraints you face in pursuing your next career? List those that seem important—and brainstorm about ways you might compensate for them or work around them.

researching fields that interest you

One intimidating aspect of career change and significant career transition can be the magnitude of the change you're trying to make. It's only natural to wonder how you can possibly get from one point on the occupational spectrum to a completely different one—when they may seem miles apart. As with many large tasks, though, even dramatic career changes usually consist of many small steps—and the key to making a change is to keep taking small steps forward. One of the important early steps in career change is finding out more about fields that interest you. Happily, there are all kinds of ways to do that kind of research.

Hear the word *research*, and you may think of combing through shelves and shelves of books in a remote corner of some library—or spending hours and hours searching obscure databases online. And indeed, research using written sources can be invaluable to career-changers—as Teresa Bell's story in chapter 10 illustrates. But there are also other ways to research potential new career directions.

Consider the story of Chris Gardner, whose career change from medical equipment salesman to successful stockbroker and, ultimately, successful entrepreneur is told in his memoir *The Pursuit of Happyness*.

(Gardner's story was also the basis of the movie of the same name, starring Will Smith. If you want proof that people can overcome long odds to change careers, rent the movie *The Pursuit of Happyness* some weekend—or read the book.)

In his book, Gardner describes how he began to learn about what would become his new career—in a parking lot. One day in the early 1980s, Gardner was in a crowded San Francisco parking lot where his car was parked. Parking spots can be hard to come by in cities like San Francisco, and Gardner saw an elegantly dressed man in a beautiful, expensive sports car driving slowly around the lot, looking unsuccessfully for a parking space. It was a time when Gardner was eager to earn more money in his work life, and he took a bold step. He approached the man driving the sports car and offered to give him his own parking space—in exchange for the answer to a few questions. The man in the car agreed to this, and Gardner asked him two questions: what he did for a living and how he did it.[1] The stranger, laughing, answered that he was a stockbroker, and he agreed to meet Gardner for lunch several weeks later to talk about his profession.

Over lunch, Gardner learned about what a stockbroker does, and he realized that the job required some of the same types of sales skills he used in his own work as a medical equipment salesperson. The stockbroker explained that Gardner's lack of a college degree would make it harder for him to break into the field, but that some companies had training programs that he could apply for without a college degree. However, he would ultimately have to take an exam to earn a license before he could become a stockbroker. And that's what Gardner did.[2]

Although unusual, experiences like Gardner's are not as completely out of the ordinary as you might think. More than one of the career-changers I interviewed indicated that chance encounters with strangers—in other words, the kind of conversations that involve asking people you meet about the work they do or telling them about the kind of job you are looking for—played an important role in helping them in a career transition. For instance, Robin Flint bought a piano, and the purchase included a free tuning. Flint began to talk to the woman who came to tune the piano and ask her questions—and Flint subsequently became a piano technician.

a variety of research methods

In truth, the career-changers I interviewed used a wide range of techniques to learn more about the fields that interested them, with different people using different approaches. Here are a variety of ways people learned more about the fields that interested them:

- Using the career reference section at the local library or using the Internet to do research about a potential career.

- Finding an industry or professional association. Whether you're interested in becoming an electrical inspector, a professional organizer who helps people deal with clutter, or the owner of a farm equipment dealership—or anything in between—there may be an industry or professional association of people who do just that. Such associations can be great sources of information and trends about a particular field. National associations may have good information on industry trends; state or local chapters (or regional associations) may know the most about resources in your local area. Local chapters or state or regional associations can be a good way to make contacts in a field that's new to you.

- Reading about a career option—whether through books or through magazines about a particular profession or industry.

- Going to events, such as trade shows, conferences, or local events where people in the industry congregate.

- Talking to people you know who do the kind of work you are interested in.

- Talking to people you meet who do or have done work that interests you.

- Talking to people who, although not actually working in the occupation you wish to enter, are in a related field or have knowledge of it.

- Through people you know, getting referrals to people you don't yet know in careers or industries that interest you; conducting a series of informational interviews to learn more about a particular profession or professions.

- Learning more about an occupation through hands-on experiences, such as an internship, part-time job, or short course. (We'll discuss approaches like those further in chapter 13.)

exploring alternatives

Each person's research process will be different, and how long it takes will vary depending on your circumstances. For example, if you are researching new careers while out of work, you can probably move more quickly than if you are busy with a full-time job while researching. And it's perfectly normal to look into more than one career option at once—in fact, it may be desirable to do so unless you are really clear on the direction you want to follow. (You probably, however, want to seriously explore only a few potential career directions at a time—or you're apt to scatter your energies.) In *Working Identity*, a fascinating book on career change, Herminia Ibarra studied mid-career professionals who changed careers. She concluded that, for such career-changers, an important part of the process is testing and exploring multiple possible new career identities, which she calls "possible selves." According to Ibarra, rather than trying to figure out up front what the next ideal career for you is (something she calls the "plan-and-implement model"

> It's perfectly normal to look into more than one career option at once—in fact, it may be desirable to do so unless you are really clear on the direction you want to follow.

of career reinvention), it makes sense to start to explore a number of career alternatives that interest you—and see what you learn from your explorations (a process she calls the "test-and-learn model").[3]

Research—particularly if it combines gaining knowledge about the field with making connections with people in it—is a great first step to exploring possible career options. It's also a great way to take the daunting task of career change and break it down into manageable next steps. Give yourself mental freedom to explore, to learn, to find out what sounds good about another occupation and what doesn't.

To be fair, I should point out that a number of the successful career-changers I interviewed didn't really do formal research about one or more career options; some got into their next career as an opportunity presented itself, or their new work evolved out of something they were already doing or already knew something about. However, because one reason career changes can fail is that people find they can't make it in a new field (whether due to job scarcity or just an inability to earn enough money in an enjoyable but financially challenging profession), it just makes sense to do some research into any new career you're considering. You can use a variety of approaches, and the Internet makes starting your research much easier than it used to be.

resources

The *Occupational Outlook Handbook*, produced by the U.S. Bureau of Labor Statistics, contains valuable information about many common occupations. It's available free online at www.bls.gov/OCO/ and can also be purchased as a print edition.

Ask your local librarian what career reference books and resources your library has available.

The *Encyclopedia of Associations*, published by Gale, lists more than twenty-five thousand different organizations and is available in some libraries.

You can do preliminary research about careers that interest you both by talking to people and by reading. In the next chapter, we'll focus on the people part of the equation—but it's often helpful to start with some reading, as that will give you background information that can inform your conversations.

So pick one or more occupations that particularly interest you and do some research about them, using the Internet or the library—or, ideally, both. (If you find library research intimidating—or you aren't finding what you need—ask a librarian in your local public library to help you.) A great place to start your research—particularly if you have a fairly common type of occupation in mind—is the U.S. Bureau of Labor Statistics' ***Occupational Outlook Handbook***, which has a print edition but is also available online at www.bls.gov/OCO/; it contains detailed information about numerous careers, ranging from veterinary technician to surveyor to food service manager. (If, however, your aim is to do something fairly unusual or not easily identified by a common job description—say, starting a business selling high-end dog biscuits—the *Occupational Outlook Handbook* may be less helpful. You may be better off starting your research with an Internet search engine such as Google.) Another good resource is the website **www.careeronestop.org**, described in chapter 8 and chapter 9.

During this phase of your research, try to find answers to as many of the following questions as you can, as well as to any other questions that are important to you. Take notes in your career change journal on what you find and print out, photocopy, or save helpful documents. And if you can't answer all of the following questions through Internet and library research alone, don't worry; in the next chapter you'll get a chance to try another kind of research that can give you important answers: talking to people.

1. Can you find one or more industry or professional associations that serve people in the occupation that interests you or a related occupation? If you can, what can you learn by visiting the association's website?

2. Can you identify a publication (such as a specialized magazine or newsletter) that relates to this occupation? Specialized publications are a great way to learn about trends affecting a field.

3. What kind of training, licensing, or education is typical for people who work in this occupation? Are there exceptions, or is this type of training, licensing, or education required by law?

4. How is the job market for this occupation right now? Is it projected to grow or decline over time?

5. What are some of the key skills and requirements for doing this kind of work well?

6. What are typical earnings in this occupation like?

7. What are some of the settings in which people in this occupation typically work (for example, outdoors, at customers' homes, in an office, in a hospital or nursing home)?

8. What else can you find out about what the work is like?

CHAPTER 12

people power

You've identified several possible career directions you'd like to explore—and done some preliminary research about them, using the Internet or the library. You've thought about your own life goals, your strengths and limitations, and your personal and financial situation. Now you're ready to take the next steps to further explore one or more career directions.

At some point, that usually means talking to people—either people you already know who can help you, or people you haven't yet met who know about the career that interests you. Now, if you're like many people, you may cringe at the word *networking*. The concept has something of an image problem. It may make you think of standing in a room full of strangers, handing out business cards—and that is indeed one definition of "networking." Or maybe the word brings to mind the kind of networks of powerful contacts that you imagine are enjoyed only by people who are born rich and privileged or who went to high-powered schools. Based on these preconceptions, the prospect of networking can seem either intimidating or not useful in your own situation.

But the truth is, we all have existing networks—whether of friends, family, colleagues, former colleagues, neighbors and community members, former classmates, members of a religious group we're part of, members of a professional association we're part of, or people with whom we do any type of volunteer or recreational activity. And there are additional networks that you may discover—and possibly join—as you explore new career directions.

Career change is not generally a solitary activity. People who successfully change careers often do so with help from other people they know or come to know. In fact, *networking with others*—whether called that or not—was a common theme in many of the stories I heard when interviewing career-changers. People who successfully change careers often use one or both of two types of networking: (1) obtaining a specific kind of help from someone in their existing networks of relationships or (2) networking with new people to learn and gain more information. Let's discuss each type of networking separately.

> People who successfully change careers often do so with help from other people they know or come to know.

putting your existing networks to work

At some point in your career change, you are likely to need some kind of assistance. And you are much more likely to get that help if you are willing to seek it out from others. Indeed, the help you need could come from just about anyone you know. It doesn't necessarily have to come from people who are especially powerful or well connected; it could come from family, friends, people you know or meet in your community, colleagues or former colleagues. Here are several examples that illustrate the power of ordinary people's existing networks to help in career change:

- **A relative.** When Greg McCormick was changing careers from working in construction to becoming a physician assistant (PA), he got some unanticipated help from a relative: his aunt. McCormick had just completed his graduate school training for his new career, had obtained his license, and was looking for his first job in his new profession. McCormick's aunt was accompanying his grandmother to an appointment with a surgeon, and the aunt asked the surgeon if he knew of any job openings for PAs. It turned out the doctor did—because he himself was looking for a PA. After interviewing, McCormick ended up getting his first job as a PA—with his grandmother's doctor.

- **Another person working in the same large organization.** When the large high-tech company where Ellin Hanlon worked was being acquired, the company offered a career development seminar for employees. As part of the seminar, Hanlon made a presentation about her idea to start a landscape design business—pursuing a longtime hobby and love. Afterward, another woman in the seminar encouraged Hanlon and told her to be in touch if she started the garden design business. After Hanlon's job was eliminated following the merger, Hanlon did start a garden design business. At that point, she recalled, she wrote a letter to "everyone I knew, announcing that I was starting my own business." One of the people to whom Hanlon sent the letter was the former colleague who had encouraged her. That former coworker called right away, and she and her husband became Hanlon's first clients in her new business.

- **Significant other's hairdresser.** When Robyn Michaels wanted to start a retail store, she had a problem: finding a good retail space that she could afford. What's more, many commercial landlords in the neighborhoods where she wanted to locate weren't willing to rent to a fledgling start-up business. In her spare time, Michaels looked and looked for the right space—for about five years. Then one day Michaels's life partner, Joanne, was at the hairdresser's getting her hair cut—and learned that the hair salon was moving. Joanne passed that information on to Michaels, who contacted the landlord of the space soon to be vacated by the beauty salon. The upshot? Michaels got a retail space she could afford, before it was ever advertised.

Chances are that, whether you are aware of it or not, there are networks of people already in your life who can help you—although it's often hard to know in advance who will provide the essential piece of information or support your need. One key to getting help? Being as open as you can about what you are looking for. You never know who may be able to help you.

networking to learn

In all the cases I just described, people were helped by people in their existing networks, such as family, colleagues, or people in the same community. That kind of networking is important for career-changers—and often for people simply changing jobs in the same field, too. But there is a second type of networking that is particularly important for people who want to change careers. Think of it as *networking to learn*.

If you want to embark on a new career, your chances of doing that successfully will improve if you can identify and talk to people already in that field. Through them, you can learn invaluable information, such as what kind of preparation you need, how to get it, what strategies to pursue, and what pitfalls to avoid. And what's more, you may meet people who can help you get started in the new field.

How do you go about doing that kind of networking? Here are several examples of people who successfully networked to learn about new professions:

Ask people who are already in the field for information or advice. When Carol Tienken left her employer of many years after the area of the company where she was working was cut back, she wasn't sure what kind of work she wanted to do next. So she conducted dozens of informational interviews with people who worked in a variety of fields that interested her. Although informational interviews are generally for learning about an industry rather than for seeking a job, in Tienken's case one of those interviews led directly to her next career. During an informational interview with the CEO of a nonprofit food bank,

Tienken learned that the organization had an opening for a chief operating officer. She applied for and got the job. All in all, Tienken said, she conducted about fifty informational interviews, talking with people about the work they did. An added benefit: she enjoyed the conversations. "I really can't think of one informational interview that wasn't incredibly fascinating," Tienken said.

Seek out associations, conferences, or educational nonprofits in the industry you want to enter. When Jim Pitts, a district sales manager at a high-tech company, began to think he might want to change careers and become an organic farmer, he started attending conferences and seminars put on by an organic farming association in his region, the Northeast Organic Farming Association (NOFA). While some of the farmers Pitts spoke with were skeptical of his plans, others were extremely helpful, he recalled. He also found out about a nonprofit in his area that offered training in farming—the New England Small Farm Institute (www.smallfarm.org). Meanwhile, in the early 1990s, Pitts's corporate employer began downsizing substantially. In 1994, the part of the organization in which he worked had its funding withdrawn. So Pitts left the corporate world and became an organic farmer; he runs Delta Organic Farm and Bed & Breakfast.

Seek out advice about your new endeavor. After one woman was laid off from her job, she ended up starting a catering company. When she was launching the business, she sought out help from a local Small Business Development Center (SBDC). There she got assistance in areas such as understanding business financial statements. (For more information about SBDCs and how to find them, see the Resources section in chapter 16.)

Seek feedback about your new strategy—before you begin. When Duncan McDougall was changing careers from working as a management consultant to starting a nonprofit, he left his full-time consulting job and began working about half-time as an independent consultant to pay the bills. He used the rest of his time to research his idea for starting a nonprofit to encourage a love of reading among children in Vermont and New Hampshire. In his research, McDougall talked to people in those two states who were involved in literacy, libraries, or related areas. He started with a list of about twenty people to contact. When he spoke with a person, MacDougall would describe his idea and then ask several questions: if there were any organizations doing similar work, if there was a need for the organization he had in mind, and if there was anyone else he should talk to.

After about six months of this research, McDougall had spoken to more than two hundred individuals. The feedback McDougall got was positive. Out of all the people he contacted, he came up with a list of twenty-four people who had seemed particularly interested in being involved in his nonprofit concept. He invited those twenty-four people to come to an inaugural brainstorming meeting; eighteen were able to come. The month after that inaugural meeting, the Children's Literacy Foundation (www.clifonline.org) was launched, and most of the people who were at the inaugural meeting became members of the new nonprofit's board of directors or its advisory board.

barriers to asking for help

It's one thing to understand that asking others for help will increase your likelihood of success in changing careers—and it's another thing to actually go do it. Some people have no problem asking others in their network for help or seeking out new networks of people. However, others may find the prospect daunting. There can be a lot of emotional barriers to asking for help: shyness, fear of appearing stupid, fear of being rejected—or just plain unwillingness to appear vulnerable.

If you feel hampered by any of those emotions, consider the following insight. In her book *Wishcraft*, career counselor Barbara Sher makes an excellent point: most people like to help with specific, strategic problems that they can easily help solve (as opposed to, say, emotional issues).[1] In another of her books, Sher suggests the following approach: Tell other people about a wish you have and then about the obstacle you face to achieving your wish. According to Sher, humans are such natural problem-solvers that people will start trying to solve your problem for you.[2]

Sher makes a good point, in that many people have a natural desire to be helpful if they can easily do so without a significant cost to them. Why not tap into that basic human instinct to help? Not everyone will have the time or inclination to help you or give you information, but many people learn, sooner or later, that good karma is important in any career. What goes around, comes around. The person you assist today may someday assist you. You probably know that already—and so do many of the people you'll be asking for help. So there's a good chance that some of them will help you in that same spirit.

---

resources

One book on networking that is well worth reading is **Never Eat Alone and Other Secrets to Success, One Relationship at a Time** by Keith Ferrazzi, with Tahl Raz (New York: Doubleday, 2005). If there were black belts in networking, entrepreneur Keith Ferrazzi would have one. You may not want to spend quite as much time and energy on the art of professional relationship management as it sounds like Ferrazzi does—it's clear from his book that he loves to network—but you can definitely learn from his fascinating book and his ideas.

Want more information about networking and how to do it? **Monster Careers: Networking** by Jeff Taylor (founder of the well-known Monster jobs website) with Doug Hardy (New York: Penguin Books, 2006) is a good, easy-to-read primer on the topic. One particularly helpful aspect of the book is the authors' recognition that natural networking styles vary somewhat by personality type—and that more introverted people may approach the task in a way that's different from the way extroverts would do it.

People in different industries network in different ways, but in some industries, websites like LinkedIn (**www.linkedin.com**) can be very helpful. LinkedIn provides a way for people to keep track of their professional networks of contacts electronically, even when people you know change companies or jobs. It can also offer the opportunity to see who the contacts of your contacts are.

There's a good tutorial about informational interviews available at the Quintessential Careers website: **www.quintcareers.com/ informational_interviewing.html**.

---

1. Are there any areas related to your career change in which you could use help from your existing networks (friends, family, colleagues)? Be as specific as possible. Not sure who your existing networks are? Consider whether any of the following people could perhaps help you:

   - Friends

   - Family

   - Colleagues

   - Former colleagues

   - Other professional contacts (for example, customers of an organization you work for, people you know through professional associations)

   - People you went to school with

   - People in your religious congregation

   - Neighbors

   - People you do any type of volunteer work with

   - People you come in contact with in your neighborhood

   - People you do some type of recreational activity with (softball team, hiking club, and so on)

   - People from whom you purchase goods or services (such as your barber or plumber)

   - People you know through your children or your spouse or their activities

   - Friends of your relatives

   - Friends or relatives of your friends

2. A key component to learning about a career you are considering is informational interviewing—talking to people currently doing the kind of work that interests you. Not familiar with how informational interviews are conducted? Happily, there is a fair amount of good, free how-to information about the subject available on the Internet. One good place to start is the informational

(continued)

interviewing tutorial on the topic that is mentioned in the Resources box on page 132: **www.quintcareers.com/informational _interviewing.html**. Another good Web resource is an article on informational interviewing at **www.bls.gov/opub/ooq/2002/ summer/art03.pdf**.

Once you feel comfortable with the mechanics and etiquette of informational interviews, try setting some up with people in the occupation you're thinking of entering. If possible, try to make connections naturally, either through someone you know in common or by meeting a person at an event. (Think you don't know anyone who works in the occupation you want to enter? Try letting people in your existing networks know what you're looking for. You'll be surprised who may know someone who can help you.)

When you have an informational interview set up, you don't want to take a lot of the interviewee's time, but you do want to ask the questions that are important to you. If you are not sure what questions to ask, here are some possibilities to choose from:

- How did you get into this career?

- How long have you been working in this field?

- What's a typical workday like for you?

- What skills and personality traits do you think a person needs to be good at this kind of work?

- What kind of training or education do you need? Do all people who enter the field have that training? (Possible follow-up question: If not, how do they get started?)

- What are the growth prospects for this occupation?

- What are some of the important trends you see affecting your industry?

- What are the industry associations that people in your field belong to?

- Are there publications I can read or websites I can visit to learn more about this occupation?

- What do you like best about your job?

- What do you like least about it?

- Do you know people who have changed careers and successfully entered your field? How did they do it? (Possible follow-up question: Do you think they would talk to me about their experience?)

- Do you know any people who tried to change careers into this field and didn't stick with it? Why do you think that was? (Possible follow-up question: Do you think they would talk to me about their experience?)

- How hard is it to get your first job in this profession?

- In general, what's an approximate salary range typical for people who are just starting out in this occupation in this part of the country? (Possible follow-up question: What about after five or ten years' experience?)

- Can you think of anyone else in your field who might be good for me to talk to? (Follow-up question: May I use your name when I contact him or her?)

find low-risk ways to explore

One aspect of career change that can seem daunting is the prospect of starting over in a new field. As you gain experience in a line of work, you come to know it and be known in it. Even a job you dislike gives you income and some type of identity in the world—and defines how a good portion of your days is spent. Because work plays such a big role in contemporary life, the task of beginning all over again in another field can seem so huge that it can be hard to figure out where—and how—to start.

> For many successful career-changers, career change is a gradual process that often proceeds in a number of stages.

However, there is some good news on that front. *You don't have to change careers all at once.* In fact, for many successful career-changers, career change is a gradual process that often proceeds in a number of stages. As a result, the question to ask is not just *How can I change careers?* Instead, also consider this question: *what steps can I take next to further my career change explorations?* What's more, if you're taking first steps, it's sensible to choose low-risk ones to start with. So the truly relevant question for people in the early stages of career change exploration is: *what low-risk steps can I take next?*

In her book *Working Identity: Unconventional Strategies for Reinventing Your Career*, business school professor Herminia Ibarra reaches some interesting conclusions after interviewing midlife professionals (such as consultants, investment bankers, and university professors) who had changed careers. Although she found that much of the conventional career advice to people considering career change suggests that they first should gain an understanding of their skills, values, and personality traits and then make a choice to pursue a particular course based on that knowledge, Ibarra's research among actual career-changers led her to recommend a different approach. In career change, "we learn who we are—in practice, not in theory—by testing reality, not looking inside," she writes. "We discover the true possibilities by *doing*—trying out new activities, reaching out to new groups, finding new role models, and reworking our story as we tell it to those around us."[1]

In other words, Ibarra found that career change is an interactive process with the outside world, in which you can, in essence, conduct small experiments in career change as you explore new career options—and in which it's very hard to plan the outcome when you start. In fact, one of the chapters of Ibarra's book is called "Crafting Experiments."[2]

test your theories

Think of yourself, then, as researching your next career direction—in much the same way that a scientific researcher investigates a theory through experiments that help him or her find out whether or not the theory is a sound one. Instead of imagining that you need to know all the answers to where you're going next in your career (an intimidating proposition, if ever there was one!), think in terms of organizing a series of small experiments designed to test various theories you have about one or more career paths you might like to pursue. As you get the results from your experiments, you'll have a better sense of which career direction seems most promising for you right now.

Interestingly, William Bridges—a well-known expert on life transitions and the author of such books as *Transitions: Making Sense of Life's Changes* and *The Way of Transition: Embracing Life's Most Difficult Moments*—offers a model of transition that also emphasizes a period of uncertainty, although Bridges frames the issue somewhat differently. One of Bridges's key concepts is the idea that transitions in life begin with an ending—a letting go of some part of one's old life—followed by a period he calls "the neutral zone," in which the next phase or direction is not yet clear and in which people often need time to be alone. In reality, the neutral zone, Bridges argues, is where life renews itself; we need neutral zones, he thinks, much as plants such as apple trees need the fallow period of winter before spring comes again.[3] Although the process shouldn't be rushed, Bridges suggests that a new path—a path of renewal and a new beginning—will emerge out of a confusing neutral zone period in our lives.

What's more, Bridges notes in his book *The Way of Transition*, few vocational transitions follow an analytical, logical process. He describes how his own career gradually evolved and how he took cues from the path of his own experience along the way. More generally, Bridges suggests that our lives develop in an organic, unpredictable way.[4]

One implication of both of these authors' ideas is that, for many people in career transition, there may be a period of uncertainty before a new career direction is clear. Not all career-changers go through such a period, however. In particular, if you are changing careers because you have decided to pursue a longtime dream, you may be fairly clear on your desired course—or at least where you think you want to be headed. But, as both Bridges's work and Ibarra's work suggest, it's not at all unusual to go through a period of uncertainty. You may find yourself entertaining several possible next career moves for a while or, more generally, being unsure exactly what to do next.

If that's the situation you find yourself in for a while, consider conducting some small experiments. Without taking huge risks—or spending more than you can afford—see if you can find some low-risk ways to take small steps to explore one or more career directions that interest you. You can then use what you learn to better evaluate the career options you're considering.

exploring in low-risk ways

What might such experiments look like in practice? Here are some examples of ways in which successful career-changers have found low-risk ways to explore new directions.

Take a class or two—without enrolling in school full-time. Karen Chartier had dreamed since childhood of being a jeweler but had developed a successful career as an employee benefits manager. To explore her career dream, Chartier first took one distance-learning course offered through the Gemological Institute of America, a nonprofit. She subsequently returned to school full-time to train as a jeweler.

Taking courses part-time also proved a good start for Ellin Hanlon, who changed careers from working in office administration to becoming a landscape designer. She began her formal landscaping studies by taking classes part-time in a landscaping design program. Although Hanlon enjoyed her courses and learned important skills such as drafting through them, the classes were expensive, and as a longtime gardener Hanlon ended up starting her own landscape design business before finishing the entire landscaping design program. Using her portfolio of completed projects, she was later able to apply for and earn a certification as a professional landscape designer through an industry association. While working, she continues to take additional classes and professional development courses about landscape design. "There's always something to learn," she noted. "You never want to stop learning."

There are a number of advantages to the approach of taking one or two courses to start with. It allows you to learn more about the field and what it entails, as well as to learn about an institution where you might study further. Yet you generally don't have to quit your job or make a huge financial commitment to take just one course or two.

Another option is to take a workshop or short course (it might be a weekend or a weeklong course) designed for people exploring an industry or career. For example, before Linda Watts changed careers to own and run a bed-and-breakfast inn, she attended a seminar on running a bed-and-breakfast, taught by experienced innkeepers who regularly taught weekend-long seminars on the subject. (One caveat: if you are taking a course or workshop, particularly one offered by a commercial entity, it should be a course that isn't just designed to sell you on the industry—or on expensive training materials to prepare you to enter it. Look for a course that advertises that it explains the potential pitfalls as well as the benefits. That was the kind of seminar Watts took. As she recalled, the course leaders shared "all the possible negatives about owning a B&B.")

Take a part-time job or consulting project in a field you're interested in. After Diane Shapiro decided to leave her career as a database administrator during a period when jobs in that field were scarce in her region, she thought about exploring her interest in fitness as a possible new career. So she took a half-time, entry-level job at a gym. Although that initial job didn't pay well, that job gave Shapiro exposure to the fitness industry as well as access to employee training programs provided by the gym. She then over time became a personal trainer, developing her skills through a combination of work at the sports club, its employee training program, and industry certification programs that she completed. Ultimately, she became a master trainer.

In a similar example, Judy Goldberger, introduced in chapter 3, had decided to leave her earlier career in nonprofit fundraising and had found it a moving experience to be present when a friend of hers had a baby. To explore her interest in childbirth, Goldberger took on part-time work as a doula (labor coach) in a hospital, assisting women who were in labor. Only after finding that she enjoyed her work as a doula did Goldberger go to nursing school. She became a nurse who now works with mothers and newborns in the postpartum unit of a hospital.

Do an internship, whether formal or informal, at the kind of place you think you'd like to work. Even if it's unpaid, an internship in a field can help you learn about how that field works. For example, at the same time that Diane Shapiro was working part-time in a gym, she had also arranged an informal part-time internship (for which she was paid just a little bit) with someone she knew who was a piano technician—because piano tuning was another possible career that interested her. Shapiro ultimately decided to pursue the fitness field instead, but her time spent learning about the piano tuning business gave her valuable information about that profession and whether she wanted to go into it.

Educate yourself about the industry that interests you; read about the industry; and see if you can attend some industry events. Robyn Michaels estimates that, in the years before she started a kitchenware store, she read at least twenty books related to her goal of starting a small business. She got almost all of these books from the public library.

Michaels also found that attending trade shows for gift retailers was helpful. In general, trade shows and industry events often offer a great chance to make connections with people in the industry you want to enter and to learn about trends affecting the industry.

If you're trying to sell your skills in a field that's new to you, try to gain experience by offering to barter. Offering to barter can make it lower risk for people to try your work when you're just starting out in a new field—and if you're good at what you do, customers tend to beget more customers. For instance, when Don McKillop was in a period of career transition—and considering changing from a career as a manager in banking to pursue a longtime love of art—his first client for his artwork during that period was his career counselor. McKillop bartered by designing a logo for the career counselor in return for reduced-price career counseling.

In a similar vein, a bartering experience helped launch Lee Finkle Estridge's coaching career. It was during what Bridges would call a "neutral zone" period—in this case, a six-week trip and personal retreat in Hawaii that Finkle Estridge took after leaving her longtime career as an independent sales rep. While in Hawaii, Finkle Estridge found a personal fitness trainer at a hotel spa who was willing to barter fitness training in exchange for coaching about launching a business. And that, Finkle Estridge recalled, is where the coaching part of her life began. She subsequently trained to become a personal coach and then started her own coaching practice.

Hire someone who is already in the field as a temporary mentor. Ellin Hanlon used this approach when she was planning to launch her landscape design business; she hired someone who was already running a business in the industry to spend some time explaining the business to her. (If you're pursuing this strategy and planning to start a small business, you probably want to find a mentor who will not deem you a potential competitor; look for someone in a different geographic region or a slightly different niche.)

Explore a field as a hobby or avocation. By the time Hanlon changed careers in her fifties, she had spent many years designing her own garden and reading about the field. As a result, when she started taking classes in landscape design, "I realized I knew more than I thought," she said.

And, of course, talk to lots of people who are already (or have been, in the past) in the industry. Use the questions at the end of chapter 12 as a resource. Keep in mind that you don't need to restrict your conversations to those folks who do *precisely* the kind of work you think you may want to do; people in other aspects of the industry may also have valuable insights to share with you. For example, when Greg McCormick, who had been a biology major in college and then worked in construction, started to explore the possibility of becoming a physician assistant, he talked with both his college advisor and a physical therapist he knew—and found their feedback about the PA profession encouraging. McCormick ended up going back to school and becoming a PA, a job he very much enjoys.

finding new opportunities, getting more information

Do any of these ways to explore a potential new career direction appeal to you? Do you have any ideas about how you might put any of them into practice? Try one. Find something small and low risk that will allow you to explore a field that interests you—and keep track of what you learn in your career change journal. Even if you discover you hate the field you thought you always wanted to be in, that's *very* useful information to have! (And it's much better to get that information by taking a smaller, low-risk step than by dramatically rearranging your life to pursue a dream—only to later discover it isn't what you'd hoped.) More than likely, however, you'll find that you get more information about both what you do and don't like about the field you're considering—and

> Even if you discover you hate the field you thought you always wanted to be in, that's *very* useful information to have!

more ideas about directions you could pursue, along with more contacts who can help you pursue them. You'll be smarter and more informed about your next career direction.

Years ago, when I was first writing for *Inc.* magazine, I learned about an interesting theory developed by a professor who was studying entrepreneurship, Robert Ronstadt. Ronstadt called it the "corridor principle." Basically, Ronstadt observed that many entrepreneurs start more than one business, and he theorized that starting a business was like opening a door and walking into a corridor, which in turn might lead to more "corridors of opportunity." Your ultimate entrepreneurial destination—the business you ultimately found most promising—might not even be on the first corridor you enter, Ronstadt posited, but it might be through some door or corridor you find only because you enter that first hallway and start going down it. In entrepreneurial terms, that meant that there might be a business opportunity—a market need—that you'd see only because, in the process of starting your first business, you were out gaining new information about the marketplace; that information might be contacts, information about good suppliers, market opportunities, and so on. Because of the knowledge entrepreneurs get from being out in the marketplace, "the act of starting a new venture," Ronstadt wrote, "moves an entrepreneur down a venture corridor that allows him or her to see intersecting corridors leading to new venture opportunities that they could not see before getting into business. . . . The key point is that this knowledge and the opportunities they reveal most often come only after one gets into business."[5]

Ronstadt was theorizing about people starting businesses, but it seems to me something similar is true for all kinds of career explorations. The new career direction you find may not be something you could easily determine in advance; it may be a door you discover only because you gain new information in the course of your career explorations.

So why not take a small step? What career direction would you like to explore—in a low-risk way?

resources

Working Identity: Unconventional Strategies for Reinventing Your Career by Herminia Ibarra (Boston, MA: Harvard Business School Press, 2004) is a thought-provoking analysis of how professionals actually change careers.

The Way of Transition: Embracing Life's Most Difficult Moments by William Bridges (Cambridge, MA: Perseus Publishing, 2001) is a wise reflection on life transitions. In particular, chapter 8, "Discovering My Vocation," shares the author's personal story of how his own career evolved.

1. Can you think of one or more low-risk experiments that you could undertake that will help you gain more information about one or more fields you're considering? Make a list of the career options that you are evaluating. Which of the techniques described in this chapter—a class, a workshop, a trade show or other industry event, a volunteer internship (whether formal or informal), reading, a part-time job or consulting project in the kind of work environment you want to be in, a mentor, experience gained from a hobby or volunteer activity, bartering, or conversations with people in the industry or a related field—might be relevant to each career option and feasible for you? Not every option will be relevant to every situation—or feasible for every person. Look for techniques that make particular sense for you and your situation, and make a list of these.

2. Now look at the list you've created. Which of the low-risk experiments you've described sounds most plausible and attractive to you? Set out, using a combination of research and brainstorming, to figure out a way you could make one or more of them happen. For example, if you think you might be interested in attending an industry event, do some research (through the Internet, phone calls to trade associations, and contact with anyone you know locally in that industry) to find out if there are events you could attend and learn from. If you think you might want to take one class, start researching feasible options. If you think you should talk to more people in the field that interests you, review the questions in chapter 12 and get started.

3. Is there anything blocking you from trying that experiment?

PART III

GETTING THERE FROM HERE

You've contemplated. You've researched your options. Now, it's time to bring your career change plans to fruition. In this part of the book, you'll learn about a number of approaches to consider when starting on a new path: the pros and cons of having two careers at once, options for getting training if you need it, and questions and topics to explore if you're considering self-employment. You'll also learn about pitfalls to avoid—and gain a new perspective on why managing career transition is a skill that can help you throughout your working life.

The goal? *To determine the best approaches for achieving your new career goal and get you started on your way.*

the two-career approach

What if you could have more than one career—at the same time? Many people do just that. Often, they have one career that pays more while the other career brings them more pleasure. For some, two (or even more) careers may be a permanent arrangement; others are, in effect, working at their old career to subsidize the launch of a new one. In this chapter, we'll discuss both phenomena, and what it takes to make a two-career solution—which I call a blended career—work well.

David Kravitz is an example of someone who has blended two very different careers successfully. In college, Kravitz, a gifted singer, studied biochemistry, but he ultimately decided not to become a scientist. Instead, after college, he attended the New England Conservatory of Music to study voice, specifically opera. After graduating from the conservatory, Kravitz taught math and science at a private school while also auditioning for roles as a singer. After a while, however, Kravitz concluded that doors weren't opening quickly for him in the professional music world, and he decided that he should find another career.

Kravitz went to law school. After graduating, he spent two years as a law clerk for judges, first for a federal appeals court judge and then at the U.S. Supreme Court, where Kravitz clerked for then Supreme Court Justice Sandra Day O'Connor.

After his clerkships, Kravitz joined a large law firm. While working there, Kravitz also performed as a singer in his spare time—and found that his voice had matured and improved in the interim. However, singing in performances and working in the litigation department at a big law firm wasn't an ideal combination. The schedule of legal cases can be unpredictable, and a last-minute development at the office could easily conflict with performance or rehearsal schedules.

After a little less than two years, Kravitz decided to leave the big law firm, and he took a job as a lawyer in state government. But while continuing to work full-time as a lawyer at that job, he found he was getting offered more opportunities to sing musical solos, and he was having to turn down some of the offers because they conflicted with his work schedule. Kravitz, by this time in his thirties, began to wonder if he should devote a little more time to singing as a profession. But how could he do that?

He found his inspiration in an article in a legal publication about lawyers who essentially freelanced for law firms writing briefs—the written legal arguments that lawyers file, particularly when they appeal a case to a higher court. Because Kravitz had clerked for a U.S. Supreme Court justice and an appeals court judge, he was very familiar with such legal briefs, and he had good qualifications for writing them. Writing briefs, he realized, was a type of law that he really liked, with schedules that he could plan around—and thus might work well with his music career. After exploring and discussing the idea with a number of contacts in his professional network, Kravitz identified several smaller law firms who might be interested in contracting with him to write legal briefs. He quit his state job and began a two-part career—a combination of both self-employed attorney and professional singer. (He got health insurance through his wife's job.)

That was back in 1999. Since then, Kravitz's legal work has evolved so that he writes briefs exclusively for only one firm, and he continues to sing professionally. He estimated that, until recently, he spent a bit more than half of his work time on music, but the legal work represented more of his income. However, Kravitz has continued to be offered more plentiful and prestigious singing work, and, in the fall of 2008, he decided to take a leave of absence from his legal work in order to sing full-time.

Perhaps even more than most careers, blended careers may evolve and change over time. Occasionally the elements of a blended career can combine—as a person who has two quite different sets of skills can be a very interesting job candidate if a position turns up that requires both skill sets. Such was the case for Miguel Gómez-Ibáñez. For many years, Gómez-Ibáñez worked as an architect and owned his own architecture firm. But over time, Gómez-Ibáñez became dissatisfied and realized he wanted to try something new; as the owner of an architecture firm, he was managing the design process and marketing but no longer designing buildings himself. Eventually, in 1997, he sold the architecture firm to an employee. Gómez-Ibáñez used the proceeds, which he said he received as a buyout over the course of a two-year period, to finance a career transition.

Unsure of his next career move, Gómez-Ibáñez entered a two-year cabinet-making and furniture-making program, to give himself a transition period to figure out his next steps. Once in the program, he found that he really enjoyed making high-end handcrafted furniture. However, Gómez-Ibáñez also concluded that self-employed makers of handmade furniture earn far less, on average, than he had earned as an architect.

What, then, should he do after graduation? Gómez-Ibáñez's solution was an elegant example of a blended career. After graduating from the furniture-making program, Gómez-Ibáñez found a niche in which his architectural skills and experience could be put to good use on a part-time basis: he began consulting to local colleges and universities that were undertaking building projects. The schools, he discovered, liked having an architect who could supplement their team's in-house expertise when they had ongoing building projects, but whom they didn't have to keep paying after the project was finished. It was a type of part-time project work, he said, "that I never would have imagined existed before it was offered to me." It's work Gómez-Ibáñez did as a self-employed consultant—and he did it part-time, while also working part-time making and selling high-end furniture, also on a self-employed basis. That combination allowed Gómez-Ibáñez to do the furniture-making work he loves while earning a substantially better income than if he had only made his handcrafted furniture for a living.

Gómez-Ibáñez had a blended career for seven years. During that period he also became involved with the Furniture Society, a nonprofit dedicated to advancing the art of making furniture; he served on the Furniture Society's board and also served for a time as its volunteer president. Then he learned that the North Bennet Street School in Boston (where Gómez-Ibáñez had studied furniture-making) was searching for a new executive director, and he was chosen for that job in 2006. For a school that specializes in training people in traditional crafts like furniture-making, Gómez-Ibáñez offered an unusual combination: an experienced manager who is also a skilled craftsperson and a graduate of the school—and who, thanks to his volunteer work with the furniture-making association, has contacts nationally in one of the fields in which the school specializes. Gómez-Ibáñez was initially quite ambivalent about applying for the new executive director job, because it is a full-time job that really cuts into his furniture-making time. However, because of his gratitude to the school that he felt had changed his life, he felt a responsibility to serve. Although he had to reduce his furniture-making time drastically to take on the executive director job, Gómez-Ibáñez continues to make furniture.

Blended careers like those of Kravitz and Gómez-Ibáñez are more common than you may think. Although it's not the norm, having more than one job at a time is not all that unusual in American society. According to the U.S. Bureau of Labor Statistics (BLS), in 2005 5.3 percent of employed Americans had more than one salaried job (or combined a job and self-employment), with that rate significantly higher in some states and regions; in Alaska, Nebraska, North Dakota, South Dakota, and Wyoming more than 9 percent of working adults had more than one job.[1] What's more, earlier BLS research suggests that the majority of people working multiple jobs work a secondary job that is in a different type of occupation from their primary job; popular secondary occupations include farming, retail sales, cleaning, and various types of part-time teaching. In certain fields, having multiple types of work is commonplace; for example, 39 percent of people who work as musicians or composers do that work as a second job.[2]

The idea of having more than one career is not new, either. There have long been people with blended careers, such as artists who have one "day job" that pays more of the bills while they work on their art, novel, music, or other second career in their spare time. For instance, the famous American poet William Carlos Williams was both an accomplished poet and a pediatrician; he practiced as a physician for more than four decades in the twentieth century.

Blended careers aren't limited to people pursuing a part-time profession in the arts or literature. For a while, one woman worked during the week as a medical assistant in an emergency room (called an "ER tech") and part-time on weekends as an emergency medical technician (EMT) in an ambulance. She really enjoyed the EMT work but could earn more per hour working at the hospital, so she did both. The two jobs complemented one another in certain ways, as different roles in the field of emergency medicine, a field she found fulfilling.[3]

These days there may be all kinds of reasons for having more than one career. The trend toward outsourcing makes it easier for people to work as consultants in their old fields while launching new ones. The Internet also makes it easier to do part-time or project work for an organization without being present there as a full-time employee. And given the decline in job security in recent decades, people may in some cases perceive that there is less risk to having loyalties that extend beyond their main employment. In a previous era, in which committed employees could expect job security and an opportunity to climb a corporate ladder and be promoted, there was more incentive for employees to invest all of their work energy into one organization: their employer's. These days, with the odds of job security at a typical organization diminished, employees have, in effect, less to lose by diversifying their career interests. Although people who pursue more than one career at once may lose some of the benefits of single-minded focus and ambition devoted to one job, they may also gain something important by diversifying their portfolio of income-generating skills. In so doing, they may render themselves less vulnerable in the event of downsizing or economic or industry changes.

Having more than one type of work also relieves the pressure to find the perfect job. In his book *The Age of Paradox*, business expert Charles Handy describes his own experience in developing a "'portfolio' approach to life" that involves seeing one's work as a collection of different projects that fulfill different personal needs. Handy discovered that, in his own life, assembling a satisfying portfolio of work projects was

> Although people who pursue more than one career at once may lose some of the benefits of single-minded focus and ambition devoted to one job, they may also gain something important by diversifying their portfolio of income-generating skills.

easier than finding one ideal job. "It was easier, I found, to make money, if that was all that you were concerned with, than if you tried to combine money making with the other attributes. Similarly, it was easier to find work that was involving and worthwhile if you weren't too concerned about the pay," he concluded.[4] Handy thinks that having a "portfolio life" at some stage of one's life will be such a common experience in the future that schools should prepare young people to learn to develop portfolios of skills.[5]

two careers, just for now

Although some people plan to keep their two-career arrangement, others choose a blended career strictly as a stopgap measure—as a way to get from one career to the next without financial mishap. For example, Duncan McDougall, an MBA who had worked for a large management consulting firm, continued working about half-time as an independent consultant for a year to eighteen months while he launched the nonprofit he runs today; at the time, he got project work as a consultant through his former employer and two other firms. McDougall's motivation was simple: the consulting work paid the bills while he was researching and launching the nonprofit.

And Lois Ford and Lou Ciercielli, the couple who segued from mechanical engineering to commercial baking, managed their joint career transition in several stages that included blending different types of work. They were motivated to start a career transition when they heard rumors that the plant where they both worked might be closing. First, in the mid-1980s, they opened a bed-and-breakfast on weekends while keeping their jobs at the *Fortune* 500 company. Then over time, based on the positive feedback Ford got from bed-and-breakfast guests about her baked goods, the couple incorporated a small home-based bakery business. In 1990, Ford quit her corporate job to run the bakery and the bed-and-breakfast full-time. After the couple's commercial bakery business began to grow, Ciercielli, too, quit his corporate job in 1995 to run the bakery with his wife. Eventually, the plant where the couple had worked for the *Fortune* 500 company *did* close, but by that time both Ford and Ciercielli were working full-time running their own commercial bakery.

Similarly, while Robyn Michaels was opening a kitchenware store, for about eight months she continued to work about twenty hours a week at her job as a community organizer for a nonprofit organization—both as a way to have income while launching a new enterprise and because she was afraid of the risk that her new venture wouldn't succeed. (Happily, it did succeed.)

Coincidentally, Michaels now finds herself once again with a blended career: in 2003, Michaels's life partner, Joanne, was diagnosed with breast cancer, and the cancer later spread. After a while, Michaels wanted to once more make a change in her career—this time so she could spend more time working from home, to be near her ailing spouse. (The couple married in Massachusetts in 2004, after same-sex marriage became legal in that state.) To accomplish her goal of working from home more, Michaels developed a blended career once again: she earned a real estate license and became a realtor for her primary work. She continues to own and manage the kitchenware store but delegates the day-to-day staffing of the store to her employees. Joanne, Michaels's spouse, died in 2007, but Michaels is enjoying working as a realtor and continues to do so.

If you're thinking about blending two careers—either permanently or as a transitional phase—here are some factors to consider:

Can the schedules of the two types of work you are planning on doing mesh? What type of scheduling conflicts are likely to come up and how will you resolve them? Ford and Ciercielli, for example, were initially able to do one type of work (their corporate jobs) during the week and another (managing a part-time bed-and-breakfast) on the weekends—but they admit it was grueling. As a consultant and a self-employed furniture maker, Gómez-Ibáñez had some flexibility in his schedule; he could be available for his consulting clients at the times they needed him. And when Kravitz worked at a big law firm, he found it could be difficult to manage the sometimes conflicting scheduling demands of legal cases and musical performances.

If you are thinking of keeping a current job part-time (or freelancing for a current employer), do you have (or can you find) a friendly boss who likes you and values your skills? Having or finding an understanding boss—and one with whom you have a good relationship—often tends to be an important prerequisite to working out some kind of part-time arrangement or scheduling flexibility. For example, Robyn Michaels felt she was fortunate to have had a good relationship with her boss at the nonprofit where she worked when she was starting her kitchenware store. Michaels's manager valued her work and was therefore willing to allow her to work flexible hours; she remembered working several hours in the mornings, some evenings at home, and all day Monday at her nonprofit job when she first opened the store. (However, the result of this arrangement was that Michaels worked seven days a week for eight months. "I don't know how I could do it, but I did it," she recalled. "I had to.")

If you have unusual skills or skills that are in high demand, there's a better chance that either your current employer or another employer—

or other clients—will be willing to accommodate the scheduling needs that may accompany a blended career. Gómez-Ibáñez, for example, worked in a city with numerous colleges and universities and had years of experience as an architect who owned a firm that had worked on university building projects. His contacts and experience in the field helped him get hired by the schools for project work—and he was able to stipulate to his first client that he wanted to work no more than twenty hours per week on their project.

Is there more than one type of work that you currently like to do and are good at? A blended career that includes your current work is probably not an ideal choice for you if you have really burnt out on your current profession and can't face the thought of continuing to do it.

Do you have enough time and energy to pursue more than one type of work at once? Are you self-disciplined and good at time management? Those questions are particularly important to consider if you are contemplating some type of transitional blended career that involves working more than full-time for a while, as you continue your old career while starting your new one. Ford and Ciercielli, for example, look back at the period when both were working full-time at their corporate jobs *and* running a part-time bed-and-breakfast as too busy. Moreover, Ford

---

resources

Want to learn more about having more than one career at a time? *One Person/Multiple Careers: A New Model for Work/Life Success* (New York: Warner Business Books, 2007) by Marci Alboher is an excellent resource on this topic.

*Wishcraft: How to Get What You **Really** Want* by Barbara Sher, with Annie Gottlieb (New York: Ballantine Books, 1979), is a classic book on setting and attaining goals for your life. For those thinking of blending more than one career, chapter 4, "Goalsearch," is particularly helpful. In that chapter, Sher acknowledges that many people have a variety of different interests, and she presents multiple approaches to developing different aspects to your life—including moonlighting and having interests that aren't your main goal but that you pursue periodically.

and Ciercielli do not have children; such a schedule, exhausting for any-one, might be impossible for a couple with young children.

Self-discipline is also an issue that people blending careers must think about—particularly, again, for those planning on working more than the equivalent of a full-time job. If you plan on working in a cor-porate office during the day and writing a novel at night, you need (1) the discipline to say no to other evening activities and (2) the scheduling flexibility in your personal life for that to be a realistic choice.

Good time management is also important. As a person pursuing two careers, you need, David Kravitz pointed out, to be brutally realistic with yourself about what projects you can and can't take on, and you need to be willing to say no to work. "You've got to mind your calendar quite carefully," he said.

How important is status to you? If you derive substantial satis-faction from having status and power within any organization where you work, you should be aware that a two-career approach may involve trade-offs in that arena, particularly if your career transition involves stepping off a traditional career path in your industry.

How will you get benefits, especially health insurance? If you are moving from one full-time job to some type of multiple-job or multiple-gig arrangement, it's important to think about how that will affect your benefits. Perhaps you are covered by a spouse's benefit plan or will be able to work enough hours at one job to receive benefits. (If not, see chapter 6 for further thoughts on the subject of health insurance.)

1. Does the idea of blending careers appeal to you? Why or why not?

2. Can you think of one or more ways you might blend your current career with another one that interests you? Be creative.

If you answered yes to question 1, odds are that you know people who have blended careers; you've just never stopped to name the concept. For example, you might know:

- Someone moonlighting, in addition to his or her full-time job, in hopes of getting a new business or career off the ground

- A friend or relative who is trying to break into an arts-related, athletic, or other competitive career and is also working at a "day job" while trying to achieve his or her career dream

- A farm family in which some family members also work at jobs off the farm in order to keep their operation going

- A self-employed person who blends work he or she really likes to do with work that pays better

All of those are examples of blended careers. Think about people you know—relatives, friends, neighbors, colleagues, former colleagues, people you know through various organizations—and list any you can think of who have, in effect, blended careers right now or have had them in the past.

Now pick one or two of the people above whom you feel comfortable talking to and ask them about the experience. What is or was it like doing two different kinds of work at the same time? What effects does or did it have on their lives?

do you need new training?

Not everyone who changes careers needs to get additional training or education to do so. In fact, surprisingly, many people *don't* need to get formal training when they make a career change. This is particularly likely to be true if you are making some kind of career transition for which you have many transferable skills—for example, if you are changing from working as a manager in the for-profit sector to a comparable position in the nonprofit sector. And if the career change you are making involves starting a small business, you may not always need additional formal schooling—although you need to educate yourself about the market and small business management, while doing a lot of research and preparation.

If you can avoid the cost of extensive additional training, there are certainly advantages to doing so. In his classic career book *What Color Is Your Parachute?* Richard Nelson Bolles describes how he gets many letters from people who are disappointed and distressed because they went to the effort of earning a particular degree, thinking it would help them get a job—and then found they couldn't get work in the field for which they'd studied. Accordingly, Bolles warns people not to assume that getting a degree will automatically translate into a job.[1]

options to consider

That said, many career-changers do need some additional training or education, or at least can benefit from some. If you think that's the case for you, keep in mind that additional training or education doesn't necessarily mean going back to school full-time. If additional training of some type may be in your future, this chapter will help you think through your options, calculate the costs—and avoid pitfalls.

> Keep in mind that additional training or education doesn't necessarily mean going back to school full-time.

If you are considering more training or education, here are eight questions to ask yourself:

1. **Are there ways to enter this career—or something similar to it—without getting additional education?** In some professions that's simply not an option due to licensing requirements. But in other fields additional schooling may be common but not mandatory. Bolles has some advice that is useful for such situations: when doing informational interviews with people already working in the profession, ask about anyone they know who entered the field without the usual background—and how to contact him or her.[2]

2. **If you are considering a career that requires a lot of additional training, are there alternative, similar careers that might offer some of the same features but require less additional training?** If you're considering a career for which the amount of education required feels daunting, make sure to also explore related fields that may require less education than the option you first thought of—but that may offer the elements of the work that are really important to you. For example, suppose your dream has always been to be a doctor, but at midlife you're not sure the many years of arduous schooling and long hours required to become a doctor make sense for you. Other options

you might consider include becoming a nurse or becoming a physician assistant.

3. **Are there ways you can get the training you need without paying tuition—whether through a formal apprenticeship, an internship or informal mentoring arrangement, or a training program offered by a nonprofit?** To pursue a career goal in certain fields, such as becoming an electrician or plumber, you may be able to work as an apprentice and earn money on the job while learning the skills you need, both at work and in related class work. And in some other occupations, you may be able to break in through an unpaid internship, volunteering, or an entry-level job that exposes you to more opportunities. Another option: nonprofit organizations sometimes offer job-training programs that might be helpful—particularly if you're not earning much right now and are seeking skills to get a better job. Ask the staff at your local One-Stop Career Center if they are familiar with any such job-training programs in your region. (To find the One-Stop Career Center nearest you in the United States, use the search function at www.careeronestop.org/findos.)

4. **Are there ways you can get training that suits your needs but doesn't involve going back to school full-time for a new degree?** This option was pursued by some of the successful career-changers I interviewed. In some cases, the training was brief but very focused. For example, Linda Watts took a seminar

resources

Interested in learning more about careers you can train for through apprenticeships? Here are two resources:

The website **www.careervoyages.gov** has a useful section on apprenticeships.

The U.S. Department of Labor's Employment and Training Administration has a handy webpage (**www.doleta.gov/OA/sainformation .cfm**) with links to apprenticeship websites (or other apprenticeship resources) by state.

about how to run a bed-and-breakfast inn before deciding to purchase an inn. Similarly, Nick Pappas and his wife enrolled in a four-day class about ice cream retailing as part of his preparation for opening an ice cream store. Another possible approach: take a semester-long course or courses that you need, but don't pursue a complete new degree. Yet another option is a certificate program; recognizing the needs of mid-career students, a wide range of colleges and universities offer these. Certificate programs generally enable you to take a number of courses to develop or enhance your skills in a particular area, while avoiding the cost, in time and money, of getting an entire academic degree.

5. **Is training while you work a possibility?** In some fields, it's possible to work at an entry-level job while training for industry certification that can earn you higher pay and more prestigious work. For instance, when Diane Shapiro changed careers from being an Oracle database administrator to becoming a personal trainer, she started out by taking an entry-level job at a gym. While on the job, she pursued industry certification and training— and was able to move up to become a personal trainer and, later, a master-level trainer with specialty certifications. Where applicable, this approach to training while working has a dual advantage: it lets you earn some money while changing careers *and* lets you thoroughly try out the career you're considering before investing in training. For more information about some occupations that involve certification and the requirements for that certification, see www.careerinfonet.org/certifications_new/default.aspx.

6. **Is online training an option?** The convenience of taking courses online (or in programs that blend online and traditional classes) can work well for career-changers who are juggling study, work, and family responsibilities. Online coursework can be a route toward some type of industry certification or a

full-fledged degree such as an MBA. One caveat: when it comes to online education, you need to do a little homework. If you're considering "distance learning," as online courses are often called, you want to make sure that you're getting education from a solid, reputable program, rather than some type of "diploma mill" that churns out meaningless degrees in exchange for money.

7. **Are lower-cost schooling programs a good choice for your situation?** Community colleges can be appealing to career-changers who return to school, because their cost is generally lower than that of other colleges and universities. And for those career-changers who go to four-year colleges or graduate schools, cost can be an important factor when evaluating programs.

8. **Is a compressed schooling program or part-time coursework a possibility?** On the other hand, the right program for you and your career goals may be at a prestigious but pricey school. Keep in mind that for career-changers, there are two kinds of training and education costs: the actual costs of the program and the cost of earnings lost if you have to stop working while in school. That latter cost can be significant. Going to school while you work in your current career is one possible course. Another possibility to consider: if you need to return to school full-time, is a compressed program—such as a one-year master's program—an option for you?

five questions to ask yourself

Whatever type of training or education program you consider, there are some important caveats to consider as a career-changer. Here are five:

1. **How do I know I will like this work?** Have you worked in a related field? Talked to a number of people who have? Volunteered in the field? The more information you have about why

this is the right course for you, the better your odds of benefiting from training.

2. **How confident am I that, with this additional training or education, I can get a job in this or a related field?** If you're quite well-off economically, this may not be an issue; you may be in a situation in which you can simply pursue your dreams. But if you're like many people, you really need to get a good return on your training investment. So before you sign up for any schooling, make sure you've done your homework. You can do that by researching job opportunities both in the field generally and in your particular geographic area (unless you plan to move), by asking about the job placement rate for graduates of the program you're considering, by talking to graduates of the program, and by talking to people already working in the occupation you want to enter. You should not simply take the word of an educational institution or training provider, particularly if you will be paying a lot of money for schooling. Keep in mind that the training provider or school, whether for-profit or nonprofit, is in essence selling you a product: schooling. Just as you wouldn't buy an expensive product based only on the words of a salesperson, you shouldn't buy an expensive education based solely on words in a school brochure, ad, website, or open house presentation.

3. **What is the opportunity cost of this training? In other words, what opportunities do I have to forgo to undertake this?** *Opportunity cost* is a term economists use to evaluate decisions in terms of other options a person would need to pass up in order to pursue a particular choice. Let's say that you have a job that pays $50,000 a year. You decide to go back to school for a one-year full-time program that costs $15,000; to do so, however, you have to cut back to working half-time and use $15,000 you've carefully saved over the years. You may think the cost of your schooling is that $15,000 alone—but it's not. It's $15,000, plus whatever interest your $15,000 in savings would have

earned had you not spent it, plus the $25,000 you passed up by working half-time for a year. That's the real opportunity cost of the educational program for you.

4. **What kind of debt will I have to take on to get this training? How will I pay it back?** Just as many homeowners in recent years obtained mortgages whose payments they later couldn't afford, it's all too possible to take on more student loan debt than you can subsequently afford to pay back easily. For example, a 2007 article in *BusinessWeek* described the story of a woman who lost her job at a call center and went to a culinary school. She said she relied on the school's financial aid advice—and ended up with $43,000 in debt, much of it at 18.5-percent interest. Unfortunately, she couldn't find a job in her new field that paid more than $8.50 an hour—and ended up at a job answering phones.[3] (That's not an isolated problem: the *New York Times* in 2007 reported that up to 11 percent of certain culinary schools' graduates were defaulting on their federal student loans.)[4]

   Before you take on any debt, make sure you've educated yourself about the financial aid process and have a sense of what your loan payments are likely to be like—and what your earnings are likely to be. (See the Resources box on page 166 for some ideas about how to start your research into financial aid.)

5. **What kind of return am I likely to get on the dollars I invest in education or training?** This is particularly important if you are going to school because you hope to earn more—or if you are thinking of spending a substantial amount of money. In your research, you want to determine the likelihood that:

   - You can get a job in the new field

   - You will earn enough that you will be able to pay off any debt you incurred

   - The amount you will earn in your new career will be satisfactory to you, even factoring in the cost of any student loan debt or the cost of wages lost while in school

Education can be a wonderful, life-changing experience, and in many cases it may be exactly what you need to help you successfully launch your new career. But, because the costs of education—in both time and money—can be high for career-changers, it's important to carefully evaluate those costs—and the benefits you think your education will yield—before you incur them.

resources

Borrower, beware! If your career change plans involve education and student loans, you need to do your homework—well before you take out loans and start school. Financial aid is confusing, complex, and changing, and you cannot count on a school to steer you to the best deal. Here are some good places to start your research:

The U.S. Department of Education's Federal Student Aid Gateway, **www.federalstudentaid.ed.gov**, contains lots of useful information. For example, a helpful electronic brochure explains the difference between federal student loans (which generally have lower, fixed-rate interest) and private student loans (which may have variable, higher rates). The site also includes a section for "non-traditional students" such as career-changers.

A project of the American Bar Association, Safe Borrowing (**www.safeborrowing.com**) aims to help consumers understand loans. The section on student loans also has information on financial aid more generally. It also explains key loan details you might not be aware of—such as the fact that it is very difficult, under current law, to get student loans eliminated through bankruptcy.

The Project on Student Debt (**www.projectonstudentdebt.org**) is an organization focused on the public policy aspects of student debt, but its website's Resources section includes advice for borrowers.

1. Do any of the career choices you're considering entail further schooling? If so, consider the five questions raised in this chapter:

   • How do I know I will like this work?

   • How confident am I that, with this training, I can get a job in this or a related field?

   • What is the "opportunity cost" of this training; in other words, what opportunities do I have to give up to do this?

   • What kind of debt will I have to take on to get this training? How will I pay it back?

   • What kind of return am I likely to get on the dollars I invest in training? Am I comfortable with that?

2. Are any of the other types of career preparation described in this chapter—apprenticeships, internships, short courses, and so on—possible options for you?

is self-employment right for you?

Starting your own business is one of the most common types of career change in America today. With some exceptions—such as people who inherit a business, or people who start one right after completing their education and training—many people who have their own business did something else before they became self-employed. Whether it's a former community organizer who started a store, two engineers who now run a bakery, or a longtime employee who has built a successful one-person consulting practice, many small-business owners made a significant career transition when they started their own business. Even when starting a business doesn't entail a shift in industry, learning to be your own boss still marks a big change in your career.

What's more, the transition to self-employment is one that a substantial number of Americans are likely to make at some point in their working lives. Statistics suggest that about 11 percent of the American workforce is self-employed, either as a sole proprietor or as an owner of an incorporated small business. Although there has been significant consolidation in industries such as farming, in which there are fewer self-employed small farmers these days,[1] other industries are more hospitable to small businesses. The personal computer, the Internet, and other modern communications technology make it easier for small, often home-based, businesses to compete with larger firms.

However, technology isn't the only thing driving people into self-employment. Consider the impact that America's dysfunctional health insurance system has on people's career prospects. A 2004 article in the *New York Times* suggested that one reason for the comparatively slow growth of hiring after the 2001 recession was the rapid rise of health insurance costs.[2] With health insurance costs in the United States spiraling upward, companies may be happy to outsource work to self-employed independent contractors, who don't get benefits, rather than hire additional employees.

> Statistics suggest that about 11 percent of the American workforce is self-employed, either as a sole proprietor or as an owner of an incorporated small business.

Today's labor market is also much more volatile than it was twenty or thirty years ago. Downsizing is a fact of life in corporate America, and layoffs are commonplace. Many people worry that their work may be shipped overseas. In today's turbulent economy, sometimes people even choose self-employment because, ironically, they see it as more stable than being an employee.

Older workers and women are two groups who are turning to self-employment in increasing numbers. An AARP study found that workers aged fifty and over are significantly more likely than younger workers to be self-employed and that about one third of the older self-employed people made the transition to self-employment when over fifty.[3] And women are starting new businesses in significant numbers; between 1997 and 2002, the number of woman-owned businesses in the United States increased by 19.8 percent, a faster growth rate than that of all U.S. firms. As of 2002, women owned 28.2 percent of the nation's businesses. For women who have childcare or eldercare responsibilities, self-employment can offer a family-friendly flexibility that can be hard to find as an employee. (However, that flexibility may come at a price. Many woman-owned businesses are quite small. In 2002, almost 80 percent of woman-owned businesses had receipts of less than $50,000 a year.)[4]

Of all the people in the United States who are in business for themselves, 31 percent are over fifty-five.[5] For older workers, a desire for scheduling flexibility (on the positive side) and the challenge presented by age discrimination (on the negative side) may be factors in the trend toward self-employment. According to an article in *Fortune* magazine, increasing numbers of older managers are finding themselves "involuntarily retired"—that is, unable to find comparable new jobs after being laid off.[6]

The bottom line? In many industries, chances are pretty good that, whether you want to be or not, at some point in your career you'll be self-employed.

That said, there are a wide variety of different ways to work for yourself. The resources you need—and the risks involved—vary widely depending on the type of business you start. From a career-changer's point of view, there are at least five important categories of self-employment:

- Transitional self-employment
- Part-time self-employment
- Full-time one-person business
- Traditional small business with employees
- High-growth business

Let's consider each of these in turn.

transitional self-employment

In a fast-moving economy with increasingly high health insurance costs, companies may be slow to hire new employees but quick to farm out work to independent contractors. As a result, people who want and are looking for full-time jobs may find themselves cobbling together contract and freelance work for a period that can last months or years. These are people who *want* a full-time job and are looking for a good one. But in the mean time they're also doing a wide variety of consulting, temporary, or freelance work.

Some job-seekers in this situation aren't happy about it. They would prefer a good full-time job—ideally one with health insurance and other benefits. Even if that's your situation, in today's turbulent job market, transitional self-employment can be a useful tool to make the most of a period between full-time jobs. As a contractor, you can gain exposure to a variety of different organizations, build or strengthen certain skills, and network effectively. You'll also get a sense of what the market is looking for—by figuring out the areas in which it's easiest for you to find work. And when you do find a job you want, you'll hopefully have a resume listing plenty of accomplishments made during your time of unwilling self-employment. (And of course, you may struggle with all the downsides of self-employment, too: You may get paid less than you think you're worth. Some of your clients may pay slowly; you may not always have enough work. Even if you're paid well, chances are good your income will fluctuate.)

For people who think they may want to change careers, however, transitional self-employment can be a very positive, helpful experience—because for those contemplating career change and unsure of their next steps, transitional self-employment represents a chance to try out new directions. For example, Ann Gray, after leaving a job as an assistant professor at Harvard Business School, did a variety of consulting projects, for a number of organizations, for about eighteen months. That period allowed her to explore new projects and, through them, meet new people. Gray had long been interested in manufacturing operations; her first job out of college had been as an industrial engineer, and operations management had been her academic area of specialty. Through her consulting, she met someone who became her business partner, and, together, they bought a small manufacturing business, where she became president. For Gray, the period of consulting broadened her options and her network. That helped her identify a new direction she liked and facilitated a career transition from the halls of academia to a factory.

What are the keys to successful transitional self-employment? You need easily identifiable and marketable skills. Ideally, you'll have either savings or a spouse whose earnings can cover your household expenses if your work flow is spotty or inconsistent, or if clients pay late. If you don't have either of those forms of financial cushion, you may want to take on a part-time job—even one that's not ideal—to ensure smooth cash flow as you build up your self-employment income. You need access to health insurance (see chapter 6). You need to be able to network extensively, both with people with whom you have worked in the past and with new people you meet by attending networking events in your industry or locality. You must be good at organizing your time and setting prices—and, depending on the type of work you do, you may need to be comfortable working alone. You need a healthy sense of self-worth that can sustain you in an uncertain work environment, and you need to market yourself. You may also require an adequate home office.

To get the most out of a period of transitional self-employment, think about your personal goals. Is there a mix of work you can create that blends projects that build on your previous experience with those that take you in a new direction? That blends projects that pay well and those that feed your soul? Also, pay attention to the type of projects that come your way: Where do they come from and what markets are they in? Which projects are easy to get and which are harder? (Hint: if there's a market in which you find that project work is relatively easy to come by and the pay is good, that may be a growth market—the kind discussed in chapter 9.)

When you are an independent contractor, there is not much standing between you and the marketplace. That can be unsettling, but it can also be an opportunity to spot growth markets and gain experience in them, broadening your skills portfolio.

part-time self-employment

Another self-employment option for individuals seeking career change is part-time self-employment. In the past, part-time self-employment didn't get a lot of attention from small-business experts; part-time businesses, because they typically involve small amounts of revenue, were sometimes seen as having little economic significance. But from a career perspective, the picture is quite different. For a career-changer, a part-time business can be a way for you to learn about a new industry—without quitting your job and risking your savings. (Interestingly, in recent years, as small-business researchers have gotten more

> For a career-changer, a part-time business can be a way for you to learn about a new industry—without quitting your job and risking your savings.

and better data about the process by which people start businesses, they are starting to recognize exactly that: part-time self-employment is often a way that people explore self-employment before deciding whether or not to start a full-time business.)[7]

Lois Ford and Lou Ciercielli, the husband-and-wife team who gradually transitioned from being engineer-managers at a *Fortune* 500 company plant to starting and running their own commercial bakery, began their career changes with part-time self-employment. When a rumor went around that the plant where they both worked might be closed, the couple decided to explore part-time self-employment—with a bed-and-breakfast inn they ran on weekends while still working full-time—as a way of opening up new options in their career paths.

Gradually, over time, Ford and Ciercielli's experiment with part-time self-employment led them in new directions. Guests praised the couple's cookies, and the couple decided to also launch a home-based bakery business. Eventually, Ford left her job at the *Fortune* 500 company to run the bed and breakfast and the baking business full-time; later, her husband joined her.

Ciercielli and Ford's story illustrates one of the benefits of part-time self-employment: it can help you explore new directions and gain more information before you take the plunge of launching a business full-time. In their case, for example, the business they eventually ended up working in full-time and growing was not the one they first launched; however, their initial part-time bed-and-breakfast venture served to give them more information and ideas about a new path their careers could take.

For those considering exploring part-time self-employment while fully employed, it often makes sense to start small. Better to take on one consulting project, or try selling at a flea market or street fair, than to take on more projects than you can handle or invest a lot of capital before you know an industry. You want to make sure that you can do the work you're taking on in your spare time and that you're not creating a conflict of interest with your current employer. You need to think about when and where you're going to work—and how working extra hours might affect your family or friendships. You also should think about your physical energy and self-discipline. Are you willing and able to work more hours than a full-time job entails?

Another group for whom part-time self-employment often makes sense is parents caring for young children. There, too, similar questions apply. If you want to take on part-time self-employment work while also taking care of children, you need to realistically think through your schedule and your childcare options. How will you juggle the time and attention needs of both your work and your children?

the full-time one-person business

The one-person business is, arguably, one of the most thriving forms of small business in America today. According to the U.S. Census Bureau, more than 20.7 million U.S. businesses with no employees (and many one-person businesses are classified that way) collectively represented more than $970 billion in revenues in 2006; that is 26 percent more revenue than the comparable total for nonemployer businesses four years earlier, in 2002.[8] The Internet and inexpensive yet powerful home computers make it increasingly possible for a one-person business to be competitive.

Unlike a small business with employees, a home-based one-person business may not require all that much capital to start. For example, Ellin Hanlon, whose story was touched on in chapters 7 and 13, changed careers in her fifties to become a landscape designer. After many years of working primarily in office administrative positions in a large technology corporation, Hanlon started her own one-person business, Bright Ideas Garden Designs. She found that—aside from the courses she took before starting—her business itself did not take a large amount of capital to launch. Hanlon estimated that, after her education expense, she spent only about $5,000 when she initially launched her business, primarily to buy computer-aided-design (CAD) software and a new computer. Of course, capital expenses vary widely with the type of business, and many one-person businesses require substantially greater capital outlays than this.

It's easier to start a one-person business in a field in which you have experience. Generally, if you're considering starting a one-person, full-time business, the advantages may include flexibility and variety in your work and, in some cases, the opportunity to work from home. The disadvantages may often include uncertainty and inconsistent work flow; lower pay, in some cases; isolation during the workday; and lack of employer-subsidized employee benefits, such as health insurance, paid vacation, and retirement plans. If you do pursue this form of self-employment, it's key to think about how you will market yourself and what kind of network you can build, both to grow your business and to provide support for you, the business owner. You also need to educate yourself about taxes and record-keeping for the self-employed.

the traditional small business with employees

Picture a small business, and one with employees is often the type that comes to mind. Perhaps it's a retail store, or some type of service business, or maybe a specialized consultancy or other professional firm. Whatever its industry, the traditional small business with employees represents to many people the American dream of owning your own business. Such a business may (and, the owner usually hopes, will) grow some, but it is not the owner's ambition to grow it into a big corporation or large chain.

However, starting this type of small business is often more risky than launching a one-person home business. That's because starting many types of small businesses with employees—such as stores or restaurants—involves a fair amount of start-up capital. And if you plan to have employees, your overhead is higher—and your responsibilities are greater—than if you just work for yourself. Also, a small business such as a retail store may have a harder time adapting to a changing marketplace than one with less sunk capital. For example, if you run a small-town hardware store and a Home Depot opens up a few miles away from your store, you face some real challenges.

That said, a traditional small business with employees is a natural model for a wide variety of businesses you may want to pursue. If your dream is to own a diner, odds are that you won't be running it alone, without employees to help. And although it may have greater capital requirements than some one-person home-based businesses, the traditional "small business with employees" model offers a very important benefit: the chance—although definitely not the guarantee—that the founder can grow something big enough to have value beyond his or her work. If you start and run a one-person consulting or service business, odds are good that when you retire or quit, the business is finished and has little or no value. If, however, you have built up a thriving, profitable business that has employees and can survive without you, you may be able to sell it. Also, with a one-person business, if the owner takes a vacation or gets sick for a week or two, the business generally stops generating revenue for that period, whereas it's entirely possible that a small business with employees can continue to function and make money.

Many companies start as one-person businesses and add employees once the company starts to grow. If you're starting a small business that will have employees or substantial capital investment from the get-go—or you're buying an existing business or franchise—proper planning is especially critical. You'll need to do plenty of research into your market, location, and industry, and you'll have to do careful forecasting of the capital required—and the income you project. You should read books about small business, avail yourself of resources like Small Business Development Centers (SBDCs) (see Resources below), talk to lots of small-business owners, and create a business plan. If you're going to have employees, you also need to understand the responsibilities and regulations governing hiring and employment.

Note: if you are considering buying a franchise or buying an existing small business, it's crucial that you do your homework and conduct extensive research and self-education beyond whatever information is provided by the franchiser or the seller. Don't just rely on the seller of the franchise or business—who, after all, is trying to make a sale to you—to provide you with information.

When you become self-employed, all the rules change. You no longer have the authority, identity, and resources that you get from the organization you worked for—and you no longer have the kind of automatic camaraderie that traditional workplaces can provide.

What do you have instead? The power of the connections you've made with people in the past—and the connections you'll make going forward. Here are some tips to help you think about building connections before—and after—you launch your fledgling small business.

Before you start, remember:

- **Never burn bridges.** Everyone you know is a potential contact.

- **Hierarchy is temporary.** Your colleague today may tomorrow be a valuable contact at another organization who could be a customer. Ditto for the person who reports to you, or the one who reports to the person who reports to you. Never assume you won't need someone in the future.

Once you get started . . .

- **Make time for networking.** Even when your work seems pressing, go to events relevant to the industry you're entering. Make connections. Always carry business cards, wherever you go. Be genuinely interested in other people and what they do.

- **Consider joining a peer group.** Look for groups, whether informal or formal, of like-minded self-employed people who meet together, perhaps once a month, to talk about issues. Some groups specifically don't want people who may be competitors in the same group (to encourage candid conversation), but others welcome people from related fields (to encourage knowledge-sharing). Make sure you feel comfortable with the group, format, and ground rules, but realize that a good peer group can offer important perspectives. Depending on the purpose of the group, it may also offer referrals or sales leads. Ellin Hanlon, for example, found that joining a networking group called BNI (**www.bni.com**) helped her gain referrals to new customers.

the high-growth business

What if your dream is to be the next Bill Gates? The dynamics and issues associated with starting a business that plans to grow large are quite different from those for start-ups that plan to remain relatively small. If your ambition is to start a business that may someday grow to a very substantial size, you need to do all the education required of any small business with employees—and more. It will help greatly if you have identified a fast-growing market in which you have some genuine competitive advantage over other businesses; it's much easier to achieve high growth in a market that's experiencing it as well. You need to think not only about a business plan but also about a team; more than other types of start-ups, high-growth businesses often develop a management team early on, to build the infrastructure for growth. Entrepreneurs who want to build a high-growth company must be prepared to work long hours and to deal with a high level of uncertainty and risk. What's more, you can expect a start-up that grows rapidly to manifest a certain type of dynamic change that is somewhat chaotic. If you don't like working in an environment in which change is a constant, don't try to grow your business rapidly.

Fast growth often requires capital. In many businesses, fast growth can create cash-flow problems, because you may be increasing your costs before your revenues grow. If you have to do research and development on a new technology, you may have months or years before your product is ready to sell. Some high-growth entrepreneurs raise outside capital from investors, friends, or family; some use personal financial resources. Others obtain financing from customers; for example, after Michael Bloomberg launched Bloomberg L.P.—today a financial giant— his first customer, Merrill Lynch, invested in his young company.[9]

High-growth companies are more likely to prosper and succeed if they have high-quality advisors who are familiar with the demands of growth. For example, if you are building a technology business that depends on intellectual property, you need a patent lawyer experienced in your industry, not your brother-in-law who is a lawyer. And although people do start fast-growth businesses in industries they aren't previously familiar with, many high-growth businesses—especially those in technology industries—are started by people already in an industry and with extensive networks and experience in it. In particular, only a tiny, tiny fraction of businesses in the United States—fewer than four thousand companies in 2007—raise the professional equity investment capital known as venture capital.[10] If you're the kind of entrepreneur who is going to succeed in raising venture capital, odds are good you are in an industry—probably in a technology field—in which you know other entrepreneurs who have raised venture capital, and you know venture capitalists—or at least know how to access networks of people who do.

Bottom line: a high-growth business is not the typical route for most career-changers—or most self-employed people. It's a route with high risks and high stress, and it requires a great deal of business sophistication and skill (and luck) to avoid failure. But for those who succeed, it does offer potentially high rewards.

Look back through the five types of self-employment described here:

- Transitional self-employment

- Part-time self-employment

- Full-time one-person business

- Traditional small business with employees

- High-growth business

Does one of these in particular appeal to you? If you're seriously thinking about a career transition that will involve self-employment, try this self-assessment. There's no "qualifying" score that says self-employment is right or wrong for you, but do take note of any questions for which your answer is "no," or that you have a hard time answering thoroughly. If you don't know the answer to a question, do more research in that area.

For each question to which you answer "no" or that elicits an answer that causes you concern, see if you can think of alternatives. For example, if you don't like to sell, are there ways you can motivate yourself to sell or gain more experience and training selling? Would it make sense to partner with or hire someone who is good at sales and marketing? Or can you set up a disciplined system to make yourself do sales-related activities—even though you don't like them?

Is Self-Employment Right for You?

1. How flexible are you—and how comfortable are you with uncertainty?

2. How high are your fixed expenses—and what kind of financial safety net and resources does your household have (such as savings or income from a spouse's job)?

3. Is the market you plan to enter growing over the long term?

4. Who will your competitors be, and what will be your competitive advantage—the thing that makes you stand out in the marketplace?

(continued)

for further reflection

5. Who do you know (former colleagues, friends, family, community members) who might be helpful to you as you seek to get your business established?

6. Do you like the work you will be doing and the way you will work? How do you feel about having a wide range of tasks in your work?

7. What new skills and knowledge sets do you know you will need, and how will you gain them?

8. Do you like to sell?

9. How can you test your ideas? What evidence do you have to suggest that your business model—the way you think your business will make money—will work?

10. Are you self-motivated and self-disciplined?

11. Have you educated yourself about small-business topics and resources?

12. Do you know how much money you'll need to start your business and pay living expenses while your business is getting launched? Do you have that capital? If not, how will you obtain it? What will you do if your expenses are significantly higher or income significantly lower than you forecast?

13. Are you familiar with the licenses, permits, and insurance you may need for the type of business you'll be starting? Do you understand the tax and record-keeping responsibilities you'll have?

14. What are your total annual income needs, including the costs of health insurance and retirement savings? Will your business provide you with enough income to cover these? How will you get health insurance coverage?

15. How badly do you want to be self-employed? If your business doesn't succeed, what are the consequences for you?

CHAPTER 17

avoiding potential pitfalls

Karen Fabian had a career dream—a career that was likely to be much less lucrative than her job in corporate America, but something she thought she'd really enjoy. And after months of planning and crunching numbers, she finally decided to pursue her dream, which involved turning a hobby she loved, yoga, into a career as a certified yoga teacher. She even sold her house and bought a condo to lower her living expenses.

Four years after launching her new career, Fabian was back in her previous career in corporate America, where she had been hired by a former employer. What happened? After several years in her new career, Fabian realized that the numbers just didn't work for her; she just wasn't earning enough as a certified yoga teacher. Although she loved the new work she tried, her temporary career change also had downsides—in terms of forgone earnings and money she borrowed to finance her transition. In retrospect, Fabian said she wishes she'd made her career transition more gradually, gaining more professional experience in her new field first—and she wishes she'd gotten more information about what most people in the field realistically earn. She still, however, enjoys yoga and teaches it part-time.

This story illustrates an important point: no one wants to plan a career change process, to invest time, money, and emotion into it—and then have it not work out over the long term. But career change isn't easy and doesn't always work out the way you hope.

eight pitfalls to avoid

However, as with anything in life, if you know what kinds of potential pitfalls to watch for—and how to guard against them—you're more likely to avoid them. With that in mind, here are eight pitfalls people sometimes encounter in the career change process, along with some ways to tackle them.

Pitfall #1: Not being able to earn the amount of money you need or want. This is a common barrier to career change. It can trip people up if they can't generate enough earnings quickly enough in their new field—or just can't figure out a way to make the numbers work at all. This is a particularly common obstacle for people pursuing a dream—a kind of work they love that may not be as well paying as other fields (in part because lots of people love to do it).

How you can guard against this pitfall: Carefully do your homework about potential earnings in your new field before making drastic changes. Use chapter 6 extensively; think about ways you might be able to reduce your spending or supplement your income. Consider a two-career solution (chapter 14). Find out how competitive your new field will likely be; talk to a variety of people in the field to try to determine how easy it is for newcomers to enter—and, just as important, how easy it is for them to earn a living over the long haul. Reread chapter 8 carefully and ask yourself: Are there better-paying or less-glamorous variations on my dream that I would still find satisfying? Would I be happy pursuing my dream on a moonlighting or hobby basis? If you are starting a small business, make sure that you have more reserves than you think you need and that you have done plenty of research. Before you take a low-paying job or start a low-paying business hoping that it will lead to better things, think through how long you are willing and able to wait for better earnings.

If you are serious about a field in which it can be difficult to earn a living, such as the arts, also ask yourself: Where am I willing to be flexible? In the kind of work I do? My standard of living? The amount of time I devote to the work I do? Think about what you would be willing to do to launch

> Before you take a low-paying job or start a low-paying business hoping that it will lead to better things, think through how long you are willing and able to wait for better earnings.

your new career. Would you be willing to take an entry-level job? Do an internship for no pay? Hold another job to support your passion? Do a kind of work that was less than ideal in your field? Go back to school if necessary? If you know what you are and aren't willing to do—and you know what others working in the field do—you have better odds of making good choices. Again, talking to people in the field before you start your career change usually helps.

Pitfall #2: Not liking the new kind of work you've chosen. This can be a real bummer, but it does happen. Obviously, the more money and time you've put into preparing for career change, the more disappointing this kind of discovery is.

How you can guard against this pitfall: Early on in your explorations, try to spend as much time as possible talking to people currently doing the work (chapters 11 and 12) and try to get opportunities to spend time in the work setting. (See chapter 13 for other ideas about how to explore a new field in low-risk ways.) The more time and money you are thinking of investing in any kind of training or education program to prepare, the more time you should spend beforehand trying to figure out if you'll like the work.

Keep in mind, too, that your happiness in your new line of work is likely to be affected not only by the work itself but also by the culture of the organization you go to work in. If, for example, you're a highly entrepreneurial self-starter, you may chafe at the more rigid culture of a larger, more bureaucratic organization.

Pitfall #3: Spending money and time on training that either doesn't help you land a job or doesn't help you land a job that justifies the cost of training. This pitfall can be a major source of frustration and discouragement. And it seems to be one to which you may be especially vulnerable if you don't start off with a lot of money or education, perhaps because it may be harder in that circumstance to effectively evaluate different kinds of training or education programs.

How you can guard against this pitfall: Reread chapter 15 carefully. Check out any training or education program—and its results and prerequisites—very carefully before you enroll. And don't forget to consider shorter types of training or alternatives to further education or training, if applicable.

Pitfall #4: Leaping before you look—and making a too-hasty career change. People who burn out on demanding yet reasonably well-paying jobs may be particularly prone to this pitfall—probably because it's very hard for them to find the time to explore new options while working their old jobs, yet their high-achieving nature makes them want to be doing *something*, right away. Also, people in such situations may make a reactive choice, in much the same way that someone who has just ended a relationship may choose somebody new reactively while on the rebound. High-powered attorneys who decide that they want to quit the rat race and become a poet or artist may not have really had time to explore all the potential downsides of their new choice; they just know they want to do something different, *now*.

How you can guard against this pitfall: Reading this book is a good choice. If you feel inclined to make an overly quick career change choice, pay special attention to chapters 2, 3, and 4. Take your time. Explore your options. Make time for yourself in this process.

Pitfall #5: Losing track of your goals while you're stuck earning a living. People who are trying to change careers with limited financial resources or very busy family lives may be particularly vulnerable to this pitfall. If your plan calls for you to change careers gradually but with a very full schedule, you may find your progress is discouragingly slow, hampered by the many demands on your time. You may face this problem if, for example, you are working at your old job during the day while going to school at night, or working at two careers—your old one and your new one—as you get started. In such cases, it can be hard to muster enough time and energy to make enough progress on your career change. (This is even more true if you have considerable family responsibilities, such as caring for children or the elderly.)

How you can guard against this pitfall: If you find yourself struggling with issues of time and energy during your career transition, review chapter 6 and think about whether you have any financial flexibility to earn less—or alternatively, any way you can earn more per hour (so you can work fewer hours). Are there family members who can help with some of your nonwork responsibilities temporarily—or nonwork activities you can cut back on to free up more time? If you sense that the problem is partly one of emotional and mental focus—in other words, if you're having difficulty making your new career plans a priority— think about whether there's a way you can build accountability into your plans. You'll gain one natural source of accountability if you can find a friend who is also making changes in his or her life or a group of people doing the same type of thing.

Pitfall #6: Starting a small business that doesn't succeed. This pitfall is essentially a variation of pitfall #1. No matter how well their owners may have planned or how hard they may have worked, some small businesses don't survive. If you've changed careers to start your small business—and many people do—you could face a period of regrouping that may be painful.

How you can guard against this pitfall: This pitfall can't be completely avoided—every small business launch entails at least some risk, after all—but the better your planning, the better your chances are. And if you can manage to test your business idea before investing too much money, you have a better chance of making a go of it. Use chapter 16 as a resource and its questions as a starting point for research.

Pitfall #7: Being unable to recover from industry or organizational changes. One challenge for career-changers is the overall fast pace of change in today's economy. It's unfortunately possible for you to do everything well in your career change process—and end up in a career position that some unexpected technological or economic shift later throws into turmoil. This is very hard to predict. And if it happens early enough in your career change process—when you still have only a modest amount of experience in the new field—it can be harder to recover from. The type of change that can affect a career-changer can range from a change in prospects for jobs in the industry to the company where he or she works being sold.

How you can guard against this pitfall: You can't completely guard against this pitfall, either; rapid economic changes are, for better or worse, a fact of life in our contemporary economy. But you can increase your odds of making a successful transition last. When you've just entered a new field, make networking a priority. Get involved in industry associations and events; make contacts outside your company and keep in touch with former colleagues when they leave. Don't burn any bridges. If you've landed your new gig without the formal credentials common in your industry, see if you can take coursework to keep your skills and resume current. That way, should changes transpire in your company or industry niche, you're more likely to be able to find another position in your chosen new field.

Also, before you make a career change, here's one question to ask yourself: how plentiful are jobs in my new career in my region? If there are a good number of organizations in the area where you could work at your new profession, you are less vulnerable should the organization where you work close, be sold, or somehow change direction.

Pitfall #8: Your fears and doubts keeping you from moving forward. This is a huge one. And in fact, it may be the biggest career-change obstacle of all. Maybe you find yourself unwilling to take steps forward or always too busy with other things to work on your career change. Maybe you tell yourself you'll never succeed, or your family won't support your change. Maybe every time you set aside time to work on career change, you find yourself playing computer games, watching TV, surfing the Internet, or writing e-mails instead. Maybe the thought of moving forward is just plain scary.

How you can guard against this pitfall: Fear and doubts are pitfalls only if they stop your progress. Realistically, anything as substantial as career change is likely to generate some fear on your part; why wouldn't it? The real challenge here is to figure out ways to work through your fears and get past them. Break things down into small steps, and take a small step. Then evaluate the results in your journal and take another small step. (See chapters 13 and chapter 18 for more on this step-by-step exploratory approach.) Start with something you're not afraid to do— for example, if you're shy, start out by researching your field online and at the library—and only later, bolstered with information and increased confidence, start talking to people in the field or going to industry events. Get support; it's easier to make yourself do something you're afraid to do, for example, if you've told a friend, a support group, or a loved one that you're going to do it. Don't beat yourself up for having doubts and fears; just work through them.

Barbara Sher, who has written a number of books on achieving your dreams, is particularly helpful on the topic of working through your fears. In her book *Live the Life You Love in Ten Easy Step-by-Step Lessons*, Sher encourages readers to take small steps to counteract their fears and emotional resistance—because small steps won't trigger overwhelming feelings of emotional resistance. And, more generally, Sher's classic book *Wishcraft: How to Get What You* Really *Want* can be an invaluable resource for career-changers held back by their fears and doubts.[1]

the benefits of understanding potential pitfalls

Don't let this list of potential pitfalls discourage you. If there's a pitfall you need to watch out for, you have a better chance of surmounting it if you are aware of it—in much the same way that, when driving a car, you have a better chance of getting yourself and your car safely past a big pothole that lies ahead if you know about its existence when you start

resources

When career transitions don't work out, people survive. But if the career transition involved a substantial investment of money and time, readjusting can be hard. If you want to get a feel for what that's like, check out these two articles from *Inc.* magazine. Both are about the experiences of launching an entrepreneurial company, but the lessons and experiences are ones many career-changers can learn from.

The article **"Hot Product, Cold World,"** in the August 1990 issue of *Inc.* magazine, is a good description of what it's like to launch a small business that doesn't succeed. It's available online at www.inc.com/magazine/19900801/5285.html. And the article **"Confessions of an Entrepreneur's Wife"** in the March 2006 issue of *Inc.* magazine, is available online at www.inc.com/magazine/20060301/confessions.html. Your library may archive *Inc.* back issues.

your trip. As you contemplate the pitfalls you could face, be realistic but cheerful; by informing and preparing yourself, after all, you're increasing your odds of successful career change.

keep your options open

One factor to consider as you contemplate career change is how easy it would be to return to your current career if you decide to at any point. How easy or difficult would it be to find a position in your current field if you leave it for a few years to do something else? And how much is your field likely to change over the next few years? If it is likely to change a lot, are there ways to keep your skills current if you need them? Are there credentials—such as a license or certification—that it might be good to maintain?

If for any reason you decide not to stick with your new career over the long term, your colleagues and former bosses could be important resources for you at some point, so it's smart to part on very good terms and to stay in contact with them. In fact, even if your career change goes very smoothly, your former colleagues and former employer may still be good resources—as customers if you start a business, for example, or as a source of part-time or contract work while you're launching your new career.

for further reflection

How likely are you to face the eight potential pitfalls described in this chapter? Use the following ranking scale:

1 = This is one I really have to watch out for.
2 = Could be a problem for me.
3 = Not sure if this could be a problem for me.
4 = This is not likely to be a major issue for me.
5 = I won't face this problem.

- Not being able to earn the amount of money you need or want

- Not liking the new kind of work you've chosen

- Spending money and time on training that either doesn't help you land a job or doesn't help you land a job that justifies the cost of training

- Leaping before you look—and making a too-hasty career change

- Losing track of your goals while you're stuck earning a living

- Starting a small business that doesn't succeed

- Being unable to recover from industry or organizational changes

- Your fears and doubts keeping you from moving forward

Now look at any categories where you've chosen 1 as your response. These are the pitfalls you've identified as most likely to trip you up. For these, you need to be on guard. Review any chapters that refer to these particular topics and think about actions you can take that will help you avoid these pitfalls. For each item that you've marked with a 1, list one or more steps that you can take to avoid the pitfall.

Now do the same for items you've marked with a 2. For items you've marked 3, think of a sign that will help you know if this pitfall is starting to become a problem for you.

small steps you can take next

Do you remember when you first learned to ride a bicycle—or to swim? Motions that now, as an adult, you do without stopping to think—like pedaling and balancing on two wheels, or putting your face in the water and floating—once were challenging skills you needed to learn. Chances are that when you first began learning them you were a little nervous. You wondered if you'd ever get them right. It just didn't feel natural to be perched up on top of that bike seat pedaling, or floating on the surface of the water, when you were used to walking.

The skills and competencies associated with managing career change and transition are a little like adult versions of learning to swim or ride a bicycle. They may well feel difficult at first—and they will require some learning—but they are important new life skills that, once learned, can enrich your experience for the rest of your life. Learning how to identify and explore new career directions that interest you— to articulate your personal life goals and values, use transferable skills, research possible career directions, network, and conduct small-scale experiments to test out new career paths—involves a set of skills that, chances are, will prove valuable to you over and over again for as long as you choose to work.

For here's the reality: career change isn't necessarily a onetime thing. In today's fast-changing economy—and era of long working lives— many people go through major career transitions not just once, but repeatedly. Often your career will not so much progress as evolve. New opportunities will come up, old ones will fade away, and you will use your well-honed skills at career transition once more. Hopefully, just like bike-riding and swimming, managing significant career transitions will become a skill you possess—a personal competency—that you can rely on to see you through periods of vocational change.

Consider the story of Susan Davy and Don McKillop. Married since 1994, Davy and McKillop recently embarked on a new phase of their lives and careers, in their early sixties. What's more, this isn't the first time that either Davy or McKillop has gone through a major career transition; in fact, both of them have had several career paths over the course of their working lives. Early in her career, Davy was a teacher and an administrator in a Montessori school as well as a mother of young children. When her children became teenagers, Davy went back to school to earn an MBA—and from there became first a Montessori school executive director and then an executive at larger nonprofit organizations such as museums, where she specialized in nonprofit finance and administration. Now, in her latest career transition, Davy is working as a consultant and interim executive for nonprofits—while also house sitting with her husband, taking care of vacation homes in the off-season. The house-sitting practice allows the couple to enjoy beautiful locations inexpensively—without retiring. And working as an interim executive and consultant for nonprofits lets Davy leverage her years of experience as a nonprofit executive while also allowing for periods of travel and house sitting. She has also, with McKillop's encouragement and help, started a part-time photography business.

McKillop, too, has plenty of experience with career change. As a young man, he worked as a computer programmer at a bank and gradually worked his way up through the ranks, earning an MBA while working; he became a manager and then a vice president. But when the bank restructured in 1989, McKillop left the organization and found himself job-hunting at a difficult time, when there were few opportunities in his industry at his level. He tried for a while to find a similar job—but ultimately decided to instead pursue his lifelong passion for making art. Combining his business flair with his artistic talent, in 1991 McKillop founded a small business making portraits and drawings of homes for customers such as homeowners and owners of country inns. That small business kept him busy, enabled him to earn money from his art—and, by giving him an opportunity to work as a professional artist, helped him over time to prepare to make another transition: to showing and selling other types of paintings he did in galleries. In 1996, with Davy's support, McKillop gave up his home-portrait business to focus on his fine art painting. Today, he continues to paint professionally and sell his work in galleries and at shows, as well as house sitting with his wife.

Although it hasn't always been easy, McKillop and Davy have learned vital techniques for reinventing themselves professionally. For example, they've each made some career changes gradually, using their existing skills and experience to build a bridge to their next positions. Davy got her first big post-MBA job working as executive director of a Montessori school—a logical extension of her previous experience and education. Her success at that school then enabled her to get a job as director of finance and operations at a larger nonprofit. Similarly, McKillop made his transition to painting fine art gradually, by starting an art-related small business that took advantage of his business skills and training. He also used transferable skills, such as his knowledge of marketing, to help him as he transitioned to becoming an artist. McKillop and Davy have also both learned to cope with and adjust to change and uncertainty at various points in their work lives. McKillop also made changes in his lifestyle, such as giving up his sailboat, when he left the corporate world to pursue art.

Stories like McKillop's and Davy's will probably become more common in the coming years. In the next few decades, our economy is likely to go through a lot of changes, and we are likely to see more and more people for whom career change is not so much a onetime life event as a recurring theme. One of the overall messages of this book is the importance of treating career transition as an experiment—one in which you take steps to gather input and information, then incorporate what you learn into your evolving plans. Ours is, above all, an era of career improvisation, with the aim not so much to find one satisfactory career trajectory and follow it until retirement as to find ways to identify and explore promising new directions as often as needed. Think of it as career trailblazing—creating a personal path in a wilderness where there was no path before. (As in any exploration of uncharted territory, you may discover unexpected beauty and wonders along your journey—and you may sometimes worry that you are lost!)

> Treat career transition as an experiment—one in which you take steps to gather input and information, then incorporate what you learn into your evolving plans.

One of the most important things you can do in the art of career transition is to keep taking small steps rather than feeling completely stuck. Remember the example of David Whyte (described in chapter 2), who decided that he would take one step every day toward his dream of becoming a full-time poet? Taking even small steps over time can lead to impressive results. In her book *Finding Your Own North Star: Claiming the Life You Were Meant to Live*, Martha Beck tells an amusing but instructive story about how she managed to finish writing her PhD dissertation after a period of feeling extremely stuck. Beck finally made an agreement with herself: she would work just fifteen minutes a day on her dissertation. Although it was a very small amount of time, it was something that felt doable—and it was better than not working on the dissertation at all. And she did indeed finish her PhD dissertation that way, over the course of a year, taking small but consistent steps—which she calls "turtle steps"—toward her goal. "Trust me," Beck writes, "slow and steady wins races a lot more often than paralyzed and inert."[1]

In a career exploration in which you don't yet know your goal, taking one step after another may mean exploring several career paths and discarding some options after gaining more information. But the basic principle is the same: if you want to make a change in your career, don't wait for a "thunderbolt from the sky" moment—some grand epiphany in which it will all somehow become clear. Instead, keep moving forward—step after step after step.

Sometimes the first step toward career change is particularly hard and forces you to overcome fears. In other cases, you may get discouraged or distracted after getting under way. For those moments, here are some suggestions. These will seem familiar—you've already read about many of them in various chapters throughout this book—and you may already have done many of them. But if you find yourself feeling stuck, consider: which step does it make sense for you to take next?

twenty small steps you can take next

1. Set aside some time to contemplate—or list, if you haven't already—what things you'd really like to accomplish in life and what's important to you. (Use the exercises in chapter 2 as a guide.)

2. Gain a new perspective by getting away from the pressures and environment of your current work—whether on a restful vacation, at a retreat or conference, or simply by yourself, alone in a place you like and find relaxing.

resources

Feeling stuck, afraid, or too busy to make progress on your career change goals? ***Stand Up for Your Life: A Practical Step-by-Step Plan to Build Inner Confidence and Personal Power*** by Cheryl Richardson (New York: Free Press, 2002) can be a helpful resource to turn to. The book includes chapters about clarifying your values, developing more courage, setting good emotional boundaries with others, and pursuing what you really want from life.

Another resource: this book's website, **www.strategiesforcareer change.com**, has additional information and updates, as well as links to online resources mentioned in the book.

3. In your spare time, take one class or seminar relevant to a new career direction you're considering.

4. Research how people train or prepare for an occupation that appeals to you; find out about any training or licensure requirements.

5. Ask people you know if they can help you—with contacts or with assistance in making contacts related to a field you're interested in.

6. Research an industry or professional association relevant to a career that interests you.

7. Find out how much people earn in an occupation you're thinking of pursuing.

8. Volunteer or work part-time to gain information about an industry you're interested in.

9. Talk to someone in the line of work you'd like to pursue.

10. Talk with another person in that field.

11. And do that again.

12. And once more.

13. Go to an industry event, such as a workshop, meeting, trade show, or conference.

14. If you're thinking about getting any sort of additional training or schooling, research several training or schooling programs.

15. Find out about growth prospects for occupations or industries you're considering; if possible, identify growing markets or sub-markets in which opportunities may be better than average.

16. Talk to someone important in your life—pick a friend or loved one you have a feeling may be supportive—about your interest in changing careers.

17. Read a trade publication, website, or newsletter targeting the industry you're interested in.

18. Talk to someone who was in the occupation you're interested in and left. Find out why.

19. Find a small way to spend a little less and use the extra money to either save or pay down debt—thus making any future career change easier.

20. Read any one of the books (or visit one of the websites) listed in the Resources boxes throughout this book.

And because career transition is an ongoing skill, once you've made a career change, you need to keep ensuring your readiness for future transitions. Here are ten steps you can take to make sure you're always open to the best next thing in your career:

ten small steps you can take once you've changed careers

1. Take on a project that helps you gain a new skill.

2. Network in your industry and profession; attend industry events.

3. Stay in touch with people who leave your current organization; they may be the source of future opportunities later.

4. Take a class to learn a new skill.

5. Read about trends in the industry.

6. Be active in industry or professional associations.

7. In your spare time and hobbies, cultivate interests and develop skills that matter to you.

8. Be helpful to colleagues and former colleagues; you never know when one of them may be in a position to help you.

9. More generally, treat everyone you meet well; remember that everyone is your network.

10. Ask advice from someone who has accomplished a career goal you'd like to attain.

And above all, enjoy the journey! If there's one saving grace about the modern career world, it's that it's seldom dull. Today's economy favors those who can grow and change throughout their working lives. And learning, like life itself, is a great privilege.

for further reflection

1. How have I already grown and learned as a result of exploring career transition and career change? What have I learned so far?

2. What small step should I take next?

notes

introduction

1. Jeff McLynch, "The State of Working Massachusetts 2004: Down But Not Out" (Boston: Massachusetts Budget and Policy Center, September 2004): i–ii, 4. For more recent information and a handy chart, see also "The State of Working Massachusetts 2007: A Growing Economy; A Growing Divide" (Boston: Massachusetts Budget and Policy Center, September 2007), 4–5.
2. William Bridges, *The Way of Transition: Embracing Life's Most Difficult Moments* (Cambridge, MA: Perseus Publishing, 2001), 140–41.
3. Ibid., 138–41.

chapter 2

1. Keith Ferrazzi with Tahl Raz, *Never Eat Alone and Other Secrets to Success, One Relationship at a Time* (New York: Doubleday, 2005), 23.
2. David Whyte, *Crossing the Unknown Sea: Work as a Pilgrimage of Identity* (New York: Riverhead Books, 2001), 115–50. For more information about Whyte's work today, see www.davidwhyte.com.

chapter 3

1. Richard Nelson Bolles, *What Color Is Your Parachute? A Practical Manual for Job-Hunters and Career-Changers*, 2008 ed. (Berkeley, CA: Ten Speed Press, 2008), 367–71.
2. Gregg Levoy, *Callings: Finding and Following an Authentic Life* (New York: Three Rivers Press, 1997), 108–17 (particularly 108–10).
3. Parker J. Palmer, *Let Your Life Speak: Listening for the Voice of Vocation* (San Francisco: Jossey-Bass, 2000): 44–46.

chapter 4

1. Barry Schwartz, *The Paradox of Choice: Why More Is Less* (New York: Harper-Collins, 2005), 3, 74, 120–23.
2. William Bridges, *Transitions: Making Sense of Life's Changes*, 2nd ed. (Cambridge, MA: Perseus Books Group, 2004), 8–17, 80–81, 133–35, 160.
3. Ibid., 85.

chapter 5

1. William Bridges, *Transitions: Making Sense of Life's Changes*, 2nd ed. (Cambridge, MA: Perseus Books Group, 2004), 65–68.
2. Herminia Ibarra, *Working Identity: Unconventional Strategies for Reinventing Your Career* (Boston: Harvard Business School Press, 2004), 121.
3. Ibid., 175–78.
4. Carol Fishman Cohen and Vivian Steir Rabin, *Back on the Career Track: A Guide for Stay-at-Home Moms Who Want to Return to Work* (New York: Warner Business Books, 2007), 139 (quote), xiii (observation that mothers going back into the workforce often change careers).

chapter 6

1. See http://michigan.gov/nwlb, accessed January 19, 2008 and January 13, 2009.

chapter 7

1. See Cliff Hakim, *We Are All Self-Employed: The New Social Contract for Working in a Changed World* (San Francisco: Berrett-Koehler, 1994), 33–37, for a more extensive discussion of the limitations of the career ladder metaphor in the contemporary work world.
2. Ibid., 33–38.
3. Mary Catherine Bateson, *Composing a Life* (New York: Plume, 1990), 1–18.
4. Richard J. Leider and David A. Shapiro, *Repacking Your Bags: Lighten Your Load for the Rest of Your Life*, 2nd ed. (San Francisco: Berrett-Koehler, 2002), vii–xi and 1–10.
5. The fruit tree metaphor can actually be used in a number of ways. One of the career-changers I interviewed, Hank Schmelzer, used the metaphor of an apple tree in a very different way. Schmelzer found that the process of career change reminded him of some advice he got in a course he took on restoring old apple trees. The instructor of that course suggested pruning some from the tree and then stepping back to get perspective. That, Schmelzer found,

was an apt metaphor for the process of rethinking your career: you need to prune out deadwood and step back to get a new perspective. See Martha E. Mangelsdorf, "Executive Prunes CEO Trappings, Returns to His Roots," *Boston Sunday Globe*, April 13, 2003.

6. Fran Delaney passed away in 2005. See www.frandelaney.com for more information about his fundraising efforts.

chapter 8

1. Joseph Campbell, with Bill Moyers, *The Power of Myth*, ed. Betty Sue Flowers (New York: Anchor Books, 1991), 146–50.

2. Ibid, 148–49; see also 285.

3. Steven D. Levitt and Stephen J. Dubner, *Freakonomics: A Rogue Economist Explores the Hidden Side of Everything*, rev. and exp. ed. (New York: Harper-Collins, 2005), 94–97.

4. See Marsha Sinetar, *Do What You Love, the Money Will Follow: Discovering Your Right Livelihood* (New York: Dell, 1987).

5. I am certainly not the first person to recognize the similarities between managing a career today and managing a business. For a good book addressing the similarity between contemporary careers and self-employment, see Cliff Hakim, *We Are All Self-Employed: The New Social Contract for Working in a Changed World* (San Francisco: Berrett-Koehler, 1994.) Another good book that discusses this topic is William Bridges's *JobShift: How to Prosper in a Workplace without Jobs* (Reading, MA: Addison-Wesley, 1994). Also, Pam Lassiter, in her useful book *The New Job Security: Five Strategies to Take Control of Your Career* (Berkeley, CA: Ten Speed Press, 2002), includes a chapter ("Strategy #1, Take Control," 19–56) that covers topics such as how to be "the boss of your own career" (p. 29).

6. Here I am indebted to the work of management thinker Jim Collins. In an insightful October 1997 article in *Inc.* magazine, Collins suggested that a company's managers should look for the area where three circles intersect: what the company stands for, what it is good at, and what people will profitably pay the company for. See Jim Collins, "What Comes Next?" *Inc.*, October 1997, 41–50. Collins later expressed his concept of three circles more fully, and with different wording and emphasis, in his book *Good to Great: Why Some Companies Make the Leap . . . and Others Don't* (New York: HarperCollins, 2001), 90–117.

Collins was, however, writing primarily about the issue of business management. When I began looking at the choices that ordinary but successful career-changers make, it seemed to me that most people considering career change financial trade-offs will find a simpler model more helpful, one that looks at just the intersection of two factors: what an individual wants to do and the kinds of work for which people will pay him or her adequately.

7. Daniel E. Hecker, "Occupational Employment Projections to 2014," *Monthly Labor Review*, November 2005, 74–77.

8. Ibid., 75.

chapter 9

1. See, for example, Martha E. Mangelsdorf, "The World According to the Inc. 500," in "Inc. 500 1995," special issue, *Inc.*, October 15, 1995, 16–21; and Martha E. Mangelsdorf, "Growth Strategies: Growing with the Flow," "Inc. 500 1994," special issue, *Inc.*, October 15, 1994, 88–90.

   One might guess that such fast growth would lead to exceptionally high failure rates later. However, when I tracked down one *Inc.* 500 class ten years later, that wasn't the case; if anything, the failure rates of former *Inc.* 500 companies may have been lower than the failure rates of other small businesses. See Martha E. Mangelsdorf, "The Startling Truth About Growth Companies," in "The State of Small Business 1996," special issue, *Inc.*, May 15, 1996, 84–92.

2. See Richard Nelson Bolles, "How to Use Occupational Forecasts," in Howard Figler and Richard Nelson Bolles, *The Career Counselor's Handbook* (Berkeley, CA: Ten Speed Press, 1999), 130–37.

3. Richard Nelson Bolles, who invented the term *informational interviewing*, offers a good description of the process in *What Color Is Your Parachute? A Practical Manual for Job-Hunters and Career-Changers*, 2008 ed. (Berkeley, CA: Ten Speed Press, 2008), 338–52.

4. The source for these projections is Arlene Dohm and Lynn Schniper, "Occupational Employment Projections to 2016," *Monthly Labor Review* 130, no. 11 (November 2007): 86–125.

5. For information about the projections of more frequent extreme weather events in the future, see Thomas R. Karl, Gerald A. Meehl, Thomas C. Peterson, Kenneth E. Kunkel, William J. Gutowski, Jr., and David R. Easterling, "Executive Summary," in *Weather and Climate Extremes in a Changing Climate. Regions of Focus: North America, Hawaii, Caribbean, and U.S. Pacific Islands*. A Report by the U.S. Climate Change Science Program and the Subcommittee on Global Change Research, Washington, DC, www.climate science.gov/Library/sap/sap3-3/final-report/#chapters, accessed August 2, 2008.

chapter 10

1. Marcus Buckingham, *Go Put Your Strengths to Work: 6 Powerful Steps to Achieve Outstanding Performance* (New York: Free Press, 2007), 8–9.
2. Ibid., 76–89.
3. Parker J. Palmer, *Let Your Life Speak: Listening for the Voice of Vocation* (San Francisco: Jossey-Bass, 2000), 51–52.
4. Michael Gibbert, Martin Hoegl, and Liisa Välikangas, "In Praise of Resource Constraints," *MIT Sloan Management Review* 48, no. 3 (Spring 2007), 15–17.

chapter 11

1. Chris Gardner, with Quincy Troupe, *The Pursuit of Happyness* (New York: HarperCollins, Amistad, 2006), particularly 1–4 and 192–96.
2. Ibid., particularly 1–4, 185–87, and 192–97.
3. Herminia Ibarra, *Working Identity: Unconventional Strategies for Reinventing Your Career* (Boston: Harvard Business School Press, 2004). Information on exploring "possible selves," xii, 23–65 (especially chapter 2, "Possible Selves," 23–43); information on Ibarra's research sample, 175–78.

chapter 12

1. Barbara Sher, with Annie Gottlieb, *Wishcraft: How to Get What You Really Want* (New York: Ballantine Books, 1979), 147.
2. Barbara Sher, *Live the Life You Love in Ten Easy Step-by-Step Lessons* (New York: Dell Publishing, 1996), 147–49.

chapter 13

1. Herminia Ibarra, *Working Identity: Unconventional Strategies for Reinventing Your Career* (Boston: Harvard Business School Press, 2004), 176–78 (for description of the author's research), xi–xii (for conclusions about career change process and quote).
2. Ibid., 23–24 (about the difficulty of planning the outcome) and 91–111 (chapter on "Crafting Experiments").
3. William Bridges, *Transitions: Making Sense of Life's Changes*, 2nd ed. (Cambridge, MA: Perseus Books Group, 2004), 4–5, 17, 128–29, 133–55, 157.
4. William Bridges, *The Way of Transition: Embracing Life's Most Difficult Moments* (Cambridge, MA: Perseus Publishing, 2001), 133–53.
5. Robert Ronstadt, "The Corridor Principle," *Journal of Business Venturing* 3, no. 1 (Winter 1988): 31–40. Quotes from 32 and especially 34. Ronstadt also wrote a more recent article that discusses the corridor principle: "The Cor-

ridor Principle and the Near Failure Syndrome: Two Generic Concepts with Practical Value for Entrepreneurs," *Industry and Higher Education* 21, no. 4 (August 2007): 247–52.

chapter 14

1. Jim Campbell, "Multiple Jobholding in States in 2005," *Monthly Labor Review*, November 2006, 46–47.
2. Thomas Amirault, "Characteristics of Multiple Jobholders, 1995" *Monthly Labor Review*, March 1997, 9–15.
3. Martha E. Mangelsdorf, "Nursing a Lifelong Desire to Work in Medicine," *Boston Sunday Globe*, November 28, 2004.
4. Charles Handy, *The Age of Paradox* (Boston: Harvard Business School Press, 1995), 75–77.
5. Ibid., 209–12.

chapter 15

1. Richard Nelson Bolles, *What Color Is Your Parachute? A Practical Manual for Job-Hunters and Career-Changers*, 2008 ed. (Berkeley, CA: Ten Speed Press, 2008), 183.
2. Ibid., 345–46.
3. Ben Elgin, "Study Now—And Pay and Pay and Pay Later," *BusinessWeek*, May 21, 2007, 66–67. This article was part of a larger *BusinessWeek* cover story: Brian Grow and Keith Epstein, "The Poverty Business," *BusinessWeek*, May 21, 2007, 56–67.
4. Kim Severson, "'Top Chef' Dreams Crushed by Student Loan Debt," *New York Times*, May 8, 2007.

chapter 16

1. Steven Hipple, "Self-Employment in the United States: An Update," *Monthly Labor Review*, July 2004, 13–23. I calculated the percentage of total self-employment (including both incorporated and unincorporated self-employment) by adding the figures reported by Hipple for 2003 incorporated self-employment (4,956,000) and for unincorporated self-employment (10,295,000) and dividing by the statistic he cites for total U.S. employment (137,736,000) in that year. The same calculation, using the comparable statistics he lists for 2002, 2001, and 2000, also yields results of 11 percent in each of those years.

2. Eduardo Porter, with Milt Freudenheim and Edmund J. Andrews contributing reporting, "Cost of Benefits Cited as Factor in Slump in Jobs," *New York Times*, August 19, 2004.

3. "Older Workers 'Pushed' and 'Pulled' toward Self-Employment, AARP Study Finds," AARP news release, March 17, 2004, www.aarp.org, accessed June 28, 2005.

4. Ying Lowrey, "Women in Business: A Demographic Review of Women's Business Ownership," U.S. Small Business Administration, Office of Advocacy, Washington, DC, August, 2006.

5. "Half of U.S. Businesses Are Home-Based, Majority of Firms Self-Financed, Census Bureau Reports," U.S. Census Bureau news release, September 27, 2006. The news release announced the publication of two reports from the *2002 Survey of Business Owners*. See also the "Summary of Findings" of the *Survey of Business Owners—Characteristics of Business Owners: 2002*, www .census.gov/csd/sbo/characteristics2002.htm, both news release and summary of findings, accessed August 2, 2008.

6. John Helyar, "50 and Fired," *Fortune*, May 15, 2005, 78–90.

7. See Karl J. Wennberg, Timothy Folta, and Frederic Delmar, "A Real Options Model of Stepwise Entry into Self-Employment," U.S. Small Business Administration, Office of Advocacy, Washington, DC, June 2007. See also Niels Bosma, Kent Jones, Erkko Autio, and Jonathan Levie, *Global Entrepreneurship Monitor: 2007 Executive Report*, 21, www.gemconsortium.org, accessed August 3, 2008.

8. "Nonemployer Business Receipts Near $1 Trillion," U.S. Census Bureau news release, July 31, 2008, and "Nation Adds 2.2 Million Nonemployer Businesses Over Five-Year Period," U.S. Census Bureau news release, May 21, 2004.

9. Leah Nathans Spiro, "In Search of Michael Bloomberg," *BusinessWeek*, May 5, 1997. See also Michael J. de la Merced and Louise Story, "Bloomberg Expected to Buy Merrill's Stake in His Firm," *New York Times*, July 17, 2008.

10. U.S. venture capital data are from the MoneyTree Report, produced by PricewaterhouseCoopers and the National Venture Capital Association using data from Thomson Financial, www.pwcmoneytree.com, accessed August 2, 2008.

chapter 17

1. See Barbara Sher, *Live the Life You Love in Ten Easy Step-by-Step Lessons* (New York: Dell, 1996), 119–43; see also Barbara Sher, with Annie Gottlieb, *Wishcraft: How to Get What You Really Want* (New York: Ballantine Books, 1979).

chapter 18

1. Martha Beck, *Finding Your Own North Star: Claiming the Life You Were Meant to Live* (New York: Three Rivers Press, 2001), 320–23.

index

about the author

photo by Gretje Ferguson

MARTHA E. MANGELSDORF is an experienced business and career writer. She is a senior editor at *MIT Sloan Management Review* and is a former senior editor and writer for *Inc.* magazine. While a freelance journalist, she for four years wrote a monthly feature on career change, called "Transitions," for the *Boston Globe*. She lives in Brookline, Massachusetts.